Cry From
Immanuel Mountain

By Ed Tuten

TRAFFORD

National Library of Canada Cataloguing in Publication

Tuten, Ed, 1939-
   Cry from Immanuel Mountain / Ed Tuten.
ISBN 1-55395-272-3
   I. Title.

BV656.T88 2002   269'.26'092   C2002-905190-8

TRAFFORD

This book was published *on-demand* in cooperation with Trafford Publishing. On-demand publishing is a unique process and service of making a book available for retail sale to the public taking advantage of on-demand manufacturing and Internet marketing.**On-demand publishing** includes promotions, retail sales, manufacturing, order fulfilment, accounting and collecting royalties on behalf of the author.

Suite 6E, 2333 Government St., Victoria, B.C. V8T 4P4, CANADA
Phone   250-383-6864   Toll-free   1-888-232-4444 (Canada & US)
Fax   250-383-6804   E-mail   sales@trafford.com
Website   www.trafford.com
TRAFFORD PUBLISHING IS A DIVISION OF TRAFFORD HOLDINGS LTD.
Trafford Catalogue #02-0986   www.trafford.com/robots/02-0986.html

10   9   8   7   6   5   4

TABLE OF CONTENTS

Acknowledgements

First and foremost, I want to thank my wife, Jane. God knew whom it was going to take to keep me in line when He called me into the ministry. She is a strong warrior of God. She is used mightily in the Gifts of the Spirit and is one of the few people I have ever met that exercises the Fruit of the Spirit along with the gifts. She is a strong-willed individual, always has a friendly smile, and never meets a stranger. Jane is not ashamed of the gospel and will share it with anyone who will listen. She has been blessed with the ability to shrug off negative talk and not to harbor bitterness. She is my bride. Had it not been for her, I would have quit a thousand times. Immanuel Broadcasting would not be on the air today if it wasn't for her encouragement when I was down and her act of putting her arms around me and whispering, "It will be all right, God will see us through." She was there when there seemed to be no hope. God would speak through her, for me to remain calm, take it easy, and not worry. He had everything under control. If there ever was a submissive wife, a perfect helpmate, and one to hold up her husband's arms when all seemed lost, Jane was and is that person. Through her own physical trials she was there all the time. If I can ever count on one person, it is Jane. Thank you, honey, for a walk to be remembered as we walked it hand in hand, side by side and continue to walk today to finish the job God has called us to do.

Secondly, I want to thank our children, Denise Tuten Barnette and Howard Tuten. They were young when the ministry began; however, they remember the days of hardship when we had to take a walk through God's proverbial training ground, which can naturally be

3

paralleled to and spiritually is the desert. Our children weren't able to have all the things their peers were blessed with. They were constantly on the go with us. They couldn't have some of the extras in school supplies and participate in activities that cost money. Going to the movies, going out to eat, having ice cream at home to eat, or enjoying a candy bar on occasion to satisfy a sweet tooth was out of the question. Neither of them ever complained. It was as if God had prepared their beautiful hearts to be satisfied with what they had and somehow let them know this was only for a season. It was as if God had placed within their hearts the notion that situations would be better in the future.

I want to say thank you to Gladys Cox. Gladys was Jane's and my first Sunday school teacher. After I was saved at Douglas Street United Methodist Church, we attended every church function. We couldn't get enough of the House of God and all the activities that went along with being a new member of a church. Gladys stood out to Jane and me because of her love and dedication to God and His purpose. In her Sunday school class Gladys taught the meaning of holiness, sanctification, and what it means to serve the Lord. She taught us that the principle to dedicate oneself to God and His calling the way it was intended meant complete lifetime submission to Him, His will, and authority. Gladys was and remains a true woman of God. Even under duress she stands for truth and accuracy of the Word of God. Her heart is God's, her will is God's, and her life is God's. Others in the church would laugh at her dedication and even whisper about her caring and loving attitude. Jane and I saw a different person. We saw a true servant cast into a world not ready for holiness and sanctification. These characteristics made her a true and shining example of those most precious attributes. Unbeknown to her or to us, Gladys taught and prepared Jane and me for the next step in our very young and immature walk with God Almighty.

Thank you to Mr. John Hodge for being sensitive to the needs of God's people. Although he was a wealthy man, he didn't store his money in barns where it would rot as a lot of people of wealth do today. Mr. Hodge used his resources for the very purpose for which God blessed him — to help God's ministries fulfill the great commission. Mr. Hodge provided the means for purchasing the necessary equipment to spread the gospel around the world. He was a father figure to Jane and me, freely giving business advice when asked. He loved us and we loved him. He has received his reward and is now in the arms of Jesus. Mr. Hodge, I say, "Thank you, and we are looking forward to the day when we will see you again."

I want to thank Terry Elrod for being a man of strength to Jane and me. No matter the situation, Terry would find time to visit the radio station for no particular reason but to say hello. He would walk into the station, and from his presence I would immediately begin drawing strength from him. He wasn't aware of this until one day I told him how meaningful it was for him to just drop by and how God used him without him even saying a word. He serves on the Board of Directors of Immanuel Broadcasting. His insight as a prayer warrior and a true man of God is priceless to us in board meetings and to me personally in making decisions and guiding this ministry in the right direction. He is always just a phone call away no matter what time of day or night.

Thanks to Bishop David Huskins. At one time during the early years of broadcasting, he worked as an announcer on WCCV and counseled individuals as needed by phone or in person. He now leads a large network of churches not to mention his own church, Cedar Lake Christian Center in Cedartown, Georgia. Bishop Huskins is a very busy man fulfilling the calling God has placed on his life; however, he still finds time to serve on the Board of Directors, imparting Godly wisdom to us in the meetings. He has a burden for the ministry and has always tried to help in any way he possibly could. David was there when very few people were. His knowledge of the scriptures and God-imparted wisdom with which he has been blessed has been useful to not only the ministry as a whole, but to Jane and me personally. His spiritual sensitivity is a complement from God for being so obedient to Him beginning in the days of his youth when he heard the call to preach the gospel.

Thanks to Yvonne Sweat for being there from the first day I announced in church the vision God had given about the station until now. Yvonne was there when we had to take a suite of rooms unused for 20 years and convert them to a radio station. It was hard, hot, manual labor, but she was there. She painted the door glass that entered into the station to look like stained glass. It was beautiful. I am sorry we were not able to bring it to the new station. She along with others scrubbed walls and cleaned floors in order for God's ministry to have a clean, decent place to call home. Yvonne had an air shift on Saturday morning ministering to the children in the listening area. She served then and serves now on the Board of Directors where her insight and wisdom are extremely valuable assets. She is always present today with a smile on her face and love in her heart for the ministry and the people it serves.

Garner "Sally" Wilkins was one of the first outside of our church I shared the vision with. He owned a cleaning company in town and had a contract to clean the drugstore after hours where I was working in the evening. He would get so excited about the possibility of a Christian station in Cartersville. He always wanted to share the vision and talk about it to the point where he would let his employees clean the entire store and we would stand and talk. Sally had super faith and was asked to serve on the Board of Directors. He accepted the invitation and played a vital role in the early years of the ministry. When the subject of expanding the ministry or simply going through hard times came up, he would always have the attitude, "Everything is going to be alright." He believed that with all his heart. He served on the Board of Directors 7½ years before he went to be with the Lord. I would say to him now, "Sally, everything is alright. Thank you for your faith and thank you for many years of faithful service."

I want to thank those who serve currently or have served in the past on the Board of Directors of Immanuel Broadcasting Network. Their efforts have been tireless. If a meeting was called, with rare exception, they were there. Guiding a ministry that has grown and is continuing to grow is tough. Hard decisions had to be made, but they were there to make them. Stepping out to accomplish tasks that cost several hundreds of thousands of dollars and no money to accomplish the task is a leap of faith. They had the fearless faith to move in God's will regardless of the circumstances. Their advice, wisdom, and Godly counsel has been God-sent over the years.

Without these God-fearing people, Immanuel Broadcasting would not be what it is today.

I want to thank the superb staff God put together to run this ministry. The staff, both past and present, has devoted their time and energy to make Immanuel Broadcasting Network, Inc. a success. The managers, announcers, and those never heard from have made a valiant effort to maintain the flow of God's Spirit through the ministry by prayer and fasting. When the going got tough they endured pay cuts and layoffs. Some even volunteered to work without pay until the situation was resolved. I honestly believe God has put together a staff that would rival any staff in the world. They work in harmony and unity to accomplish the ultimate call to spread the gospel around the world. It has been said that a chain is only as strong as its weakest link — there are no weak links in this chain.

A special thank you to all of those who contributed materials, labor, time, prayers, and finances to construct the original studio on Main Street and transmitter site on Ponders Mountain in Cartersville. Then there were those that contributed the same elements of themselves and their businesses when it came time to move the studio and transmitter to a different location. Their labor was tireless and their efforts endless as work progressed, especially on the current facilities. Literally thousands of dollars of God's money were saved by the generosity of these individuals including staff and individuals volunteering. Trying to name all of them would definitely result in leaving someone out and literally discrediting them. I am not willing to take that chance. Again, I say thank you. It would have been practically impossible from a human perspective without you.

Thank you Dr. Steven Garber, Dr. Mason Brown, and Dr. Scott Leeth for the dedication to your particular professions. In that dedication, with God's guidance and wisdom, they have kept Jane and me physically and emotionally prepared to accomplish the calling God has placed on our lives. When the diagnosis seemed difficult and healing had not manifested for either of us, a fervent prayer was prayed by them asking Almighty God for His intervention and wisdom for our healing. God used the gift He had placed in these and other physicians to keep us physically fit while the Lord was spiritually preparing and using us for His purpose.

I want to thank the following for being friends to Jane and me over the years. They were there with understanding hearts to help in the times of great need, and they were there to celebrate with us the victories. The Word of God states that a friend sticks closer than a brother. Times would come when each of these at one time or another would be so close they would seem like blood relatives. Their concern for the welfare of not only the ministry, but for Jane and I personally, was and is beautiful. I consider us blessed to be able to say that we have now and have had in the past, friends such as these in our lives. I pray blessing on those that remain and say to those that have exited this world to be with Jesus, someday we will all be together again to celebrate the victories for an eternity because the hard times and the tears will be over.

Evelyn Blalock	Connie Inman
Lila Champion	Sam and Phyllis Maybern
Jackie Davis	Charles and Kay Miller
Johnnie Graves	Patrick and Lisa Miller

Fred and Pat Harris   Mary Eliza Shaw
Scott and Holly Holder   Sandy Templeton

A very special thank you to Bonnie Ellis, Lori Hopper, Cindy Donoho, my daughter Denise Tuten Barnette, and my wife Jane for their careful and time-consuming efforts put forth while editing this manuscript.

A very special thank you to my son Howard Tuten for the cover design and to Billy Williams for all his effort put forth in locating and working with the publisher.

Some names in this book have been changed, but the testimony has not been altered.

Forward

I laughed, I cried, I rejoiced, and I remembered as I read, "Cry From Immanuel Mountain." I am sure you will also.

This book, written by my good friend and man of God, Ed Tuten, reads like a story that is impossible to be true, but it is true. Ed takes you on a faith journey that he has lived and walked.

It is the story of how God uses ordinary men and women to do an extraordinary work for His Kingdom. If God did it for Ed Tuten, He can do it for you as well. This book is a lesson in faith, trust, and miracles. Never give up faith, against all odds continue to trust and behold the miracles.

I have had the privilege of walking a small portion of this journey with Ed Tuten, and I have always been moved by his integrity, faith, and resolve. When I read, "Cry From Immanuel Mountain," I realized just how little I really knew of this journey and how lonely the faith walk had been for Ed and Immanuel Broadcasting. It was then that I understood his faith and resolve. I really believe that God views Ed Tuten as He did Abraham. He views him as a faithful friend.

This story could be your story. God may be speaking to you to "fill a void" somewhere in His Kingdom. Your journey of faith, like the one in this book, will not be easy, but God would say, "It will be a lonely walk, but you and I will walk it together."

"Cry From Immanuel Mountain" is a message of promises made and promises kept. It is a story of the faithfulness of God and the faithfulness of ordinary believers who take God at His word. This book is a faith builder and I recommend it to everyone.

You will laugh, you will cry, you will rejoice, and you will begin a new journey of faith.

Bishop David R. Huskins, Th.D., D.D.
Cedar Lake Christian Center
Fellowship of Vineyard Harvester Churches

Preface

I wrote this book for the sole purpose of giving God the glory for the things He has done. This ministry was founded on two principles: a Word from God, and Him placing the faith in me to believe a radio station could be raised up no matter the circumstances. This book is the testimony of how a 40 year-old man, only a few years old in Christ, heard a Word from God and how that man over a period of years learned to listen and believe that God could perform what He speaks. This book is the testimony of how a man and woman lived from payday to payday with no extra money and no savings, learned through trials and tribulations that God will, in His time, supply all of their need. This book is the testimony of how God called a man and woman to build a radio ministry when neither were ministers, nor did they know anything about radio.

In the early years of the ministry God gave me a book title, "Cry From Immanuel Mountain." I didn't know at the time this would someday be the book I would write telling His story of how He deals with people even in this century to do the seemingly impossible. As situations and circumstances unfolded, people began commenting, "You need to write a book." I would hear this occasionally, and each time I would think about the book title He had given me. I am not a writer, nor am I an individual that is good with words, so I procrastinated as most of us do. Years have gone by and I am now 62 years of age. Many days have passed in the ongoing ministry and God began strongly dealing with me about writing the memoirs of Immanuel Broadcasting Network.

He wanted it built for the stated but undefined purpose of, "FILLING A VOID IN THIS AREA." It has not only developed into a radio station, but a ministry in every sense of the word.

There have been good times and there have been bad times, but all the times were guided by God's hand to direct us and guide us through the maze of doubts and fears, which naturally take place in men's hearts when God's will is in the balance. To think a trip of this nature is for pleasure is a statement reserved for only the foolish. God's business is very serious business. He doesn't tolerate trite, idle, and half-hearted efforts, nor does He tolerate lack of communication and disobedience. When you are the front man, humility is the key to God's heart, and humbleness is the path to His blessings.

People have talked about Jane and me concerning the mission God called us to accomplish. For reasons unclear to us, we are still being verbally persecuted because we won't submit to the music some people like or the programs they want to hear because their personal desires are in direct violation of the Word God put forth for this ministry to pursue. They have attacked our efforts in raising up a radio ministry and our personal lives, sometimes verbally to our face and other times in very ugly worded letters, some signed and others unsigned, telephone calls and e-mails. People questioned our integrity and purpose. It has been difficult at times not to strike back, but we knew vengeance was God's. We didn't have time for the lackluster smallness of spirit to respond to these ludicrous accusations. After a period of time I began to realize people criticized Jesus in His day, and people still criticize Him today after the sacrifice He made for humanity. I was just a little fish in a very big pond. If He could then and does now withstand faultfinding, then maybe I needed to look at myself and have an attitude adjustment if I was going to follow Him. After several years, I slowly learned what it means in Psalms 2:1 when it asks the question, *why do the heathen rage, and the people imagine a vain thing?* I began to ignore such talk. God is my source and my supply. He is my Father and my manager. He is the designer and builder. Jane and I have one purpose as servants of God. That purpose is to fulfill the vision He gave us. We learned to pray for and forgive those who despitefully used and talked about us. We asked the Lord to forgive us for harboring bitterness and to forgive them because they didn't know what they were doing; they didn't have all the facts.

I learned the vision of God, that had been placed and established in my heart by Him, was the most important thing in the world, and nothing or no one, I mean absolutely nothing or no one, should stand in the way to accomplish that vision. It is virtually impossible to please all the people all the time, so you charge along on the path God has laid down allowing nothing to get in your way. If you let them, people will destroy a God-given vision and you in the process. You have to learn to be strong and bold with the assurance that under those circumstances, God is with you.

It is with and through all of this that today Immanuel Broadcasting Network is a viable ministry sending the gospel of Jesus Christ around the world with live streaming on the Internet. There are two full-power stations and eight translators on the air beaming the gospel to Northwest Georgia, Northeast Alabama, and Southeast Tennessee. This is the testimony of that miracle and this God-called ministry. This is the testimony of how literally thousands caught the vision and over the years prayed, contributed finances, and volunteered their time to make Immanuel Broadcasting Network a success. It is to their credit that hundreds have come to know Jesus as their personal Lord and Savior and can look forward to the day when not only the Lord says, "WELL DONE MY GOOD AND FAITHFUL SERVANT" but also a resident of heaven will walk up to them and say, "Thank you for giving to the Lord."

Chapter 1
Before Dawn

In January 1974, Jane, Denise, Howard and I moved to Cartersville, Georgia. I had accepted a job with Lewis Carpet Mills. A previous supervisor with whom I worked a number of years in Atlanta offered me a position with the company. My purpose was to help establish a computer department at the mill. During this time all of the company's accounting, customer service, and inventory were, for the most part, a manual system. There was some computer usage, but it was at best completely inefficient and very archaic even for the mid 1970s. The owner of the mill was interested in updating the systems, establishing new and different computer operations, and bringing a more efficient operation in the administrative area of the business.

He hired my ex-supervisor to oversee the project. I was brought on board to assist in the planning and development of a computer department with computers more contemporary to the industry at that time. When the plans were presented to the owner, he allowed us to proceed with the installation. Computers in 1974 were not the compact, ingenious equipment of today. A computer with 32K memory required a room the size of a large living room. As time passed the mill owner realized that to establish an area for a department of that size was going to interfere with his mill operation. In the spring of 1974, the owner of the mill called a few of us to his office. He informed us he was going to purchase the land up the road from the mill. We were to design and build a building that would house all of the computer and administrative operations of his carpet mill. The mill was experiencing phenomenal growth at that time, and new carpet producing machinery was also being integrated into the plant operation.

That building plan was completed and approved. In a few months the building was completed. As planned, all administrative offices and computer operations were moved to the new location. I was included in the move. My office was downstairs so I could oversee the operation of the computer department. The moving and the conversion to the new computer system were accomplished without much difficulty. The requirements of the mill and administration were completely satisfied and work continued on as usual.

At the time I was not born again and sought the riches the dollar could provide. Loving my job as I did was an increased inducement to work long hours. I desperately wanted to please my superiors by making a total success of the department, so I worked ten to fifteen hours per day, six days a week. With the passage of time the departments involved in the complete mill operation began to develop confidence in the reports generated and the work processed by the computer department. Much more dependence was placed on the staff of the department as the general knowledge of various systems increased through training and systems design. The computer became the focal point for needed information by not only the general employee but upper management as well. The entire department was operating smoothly and had become a 24 hours a day, 7 days a week operation. I was eventually promoted to the position of department supervisor and loved each minute I spent working.

In July 1974, I met Jesus Christ as my Savior and was completely turned around in my thoughts and desires, but not necessarily in the goals of my life. I had an excellent knowledge of the company operation and was very confident in my ability to accomplish any task assigned by upper management. I had an excellent relationship with my superiors and the employees. It was as good as anyone could possibly desire, but God had other plans, and I had no idea what was on the horizon.

Chapter 2
The Journey Began

It was a beautiful Sunday morning in mid-July 1974. Being home alone because Jane and the children were visiting family in Savannah for a few days, I purposed in my heart to sleep as late as possible. About 7:30 a.m. I was awakened by an audible and authoritative voice speaking these words, "GET UP AND GO TO CHURCH!!!" Believing I was alone in the house, I was shaken by the sound of a voice, fearing someone had broken in. I was extremely upset to the point of trembling since the voice seemed so near and present, yet I knew, at least I hoped, I was alone. Somehow, I felt I wasn't dealing with a human situation, but was at a complete loss at what or whom I did hear. The words seemed to vibrate inside my being, and I knew I didn't really have a choice but to go to church. It seemed to be very important that I be obedient to what I had heard. I immediately got up and phoned my sister, Nancy. I asked if she and her husband, Herb, would take me to their church. I was not one to go to church and didn't pay attention to where they were located. For me to go alone was totally out of the question. She said they would pick me up around 10:30 a.m. since church started at 10:45 a.m.

I got dressed and nervously awaited their arrival. After picking me up, Herb drove through the beautiful city of Cartersville, Georgia, to their house of worship. I was apprehensive about this entire ordeal since I wasn't sure of anything, and for some reason felt out of control of the situation. I knew I wouldn't know anyone in the church and my wife and children were not with me. We arrived at the church a little late. As we began walking the 12 or

13 steps to the front door of Douglas Street United Methodist Church, I could hear seemingly angelic voices surrounding me with the most beautiful and powerful old hymn *How Great Thy Art.*

As we reached the landing and walked through the double doors leading to the sanctuary, there were a couple of ushers ready to greet us. I began to weep. Walking into the sanctuary that seated about 300, there seemed to be thousands of people in there. The church was in the last day of a week-long revival. Wally and Ginger Laxon were leading the music. The church pastor, Pierce Norman, was the revival preacher. The choir overflowed the choir loft. The entire front of the church from one side to the other was filled with singers. They were singing as if it would be their last song to be sung on this earth. Inside the sanctuary the voices of the choir seemed to be elevated to a higher decibel than they really were, vibrating the very fiber of my being. We walked around to the left side of the church to be seated on the third row from the front. We were sitting practically in the middle. If I had positioned myself in the place I wanted, it would have been on the back row, first seat by the door.

I continued weeping, at times uncontrollably, during the entire singing and preaching. Without being disrespectful to the pastor, I remember absolutely nothing about the message. My weeping was coming from the inner part of my soul, and I didn't know why I was sobbing so deeply. I had never experienced anything like this in my entire life. I cried until there seemed to be no more fluid remaining in my body. My handkerchief was completely saturated, but the crying continued without ceasing.

Finally, the moment for which I had been awaiting arrived. Time to leave. I made a mad dash for the door having to make my way through throngs of people. They tried to be polite and hospitable, but I was in a hurry to get out of there. I got down the stairs and walked to the street's edge waiting for Nancy and Herb. While waiting, Wally Laxon walked up to me and said, "Son, you need to come back tonight. God is dealing with you." That petrified me. I had absolutely no idea what the man was talking about.

I asked Nancy and Herb if I could go home with them. I was afraid to be alone, especially at home. They graciously said I could. Nancy prepared a fine dinner but I was unable to eat. All I could do was sit on the couch and wonder what was happening. At other times I would be completely blank. Somehow I knew that regardless of my state of mind or emptiness of my stomach, I had to go back to church that evening. As the time approached I became very complacent and my mind seemed to become virtually numb.

We arrived at church that evening and took the same seats we had that morning. We were on time and the service hadn't started. All the church people couldn't have been friendlier and more caring. As the choir gathered and began singing the opening hymn I also began my crying. Again, I had no idea why but the tears were once again pouring. The crying began to subside as the service was concluding. At the end of the service, Pastor Norman gave the altar call for souls to be saved. I did not know what he was talking about but was strongly compelled to go and kneel at the altar along with a few other individuals. I made my way to the front and knelt down not really knowing what to do. I just knelt there. I had my head bowed and eyes closed but did nothing. Someone walked to where I was kneeling and asked, "Has it happened yet?" I responded, "Has what happened yet?" He said, "Keep praying, it will." I thought to myself, "I wasn't praying, I don't know how to pray and what is going to happen if I do?"

Above the choir loft was a cross that was lit by fluorescent bulbs. The light, from the back of the cross, was reflected from the cream-colored walls. I immediately began to remember my childhood. I remembered our housekeeper, Geneva, talking about Jesus, His being hung on a cross and coming back to life. I seemed to recall that we were supposed to believe in Jesus and what He did. We were supposed to ask for forgiveness of the sins we had committed. Maybe those were the words I needed to pray. Was that what he was talking about? Did I have to use words like in the Bible, which I had looked at and even read, but never understood all the "funny" English? I was confused. I began to weep again. I wasn't getting any help or advice and out of frustration started to get up to go back to my seat. I raised my head and through tear-blurred eyes I looked at that cross for a few moments. Then I began to utter the simple words, "Jesus, forgive me for my sins." I don't know what else I said, if anything. As I spoke those words, the cross appeared to begin vibrating gently. My attention was drawn more to the cross and suddenly the light from behind the cross began beaming toward me. As it reached me the beam seemingly touched the center of my chest. In that instant, I felt the cares and burdens, which I didn't know I had, leave as if someone had literally snatched them from within my innermost being. It was as if someone had taken a strong soap and

23

completely washed me clean from the inside to the outside. In an instant I felt like a completely different person. I didn't know what had happened, but it was certainly different. It was wonderful. I jumped up from the altar and began running to my seat. I threw my right arm up in the air and shouted "Hallelujah!" I had joy pouring out of the depths of my soul. I truly didn't know what had happened, but I knew I was not the same person that walked into Douglas Street United Methodist an hour earlier. I did not know that you weren't supposed to shout in a Methodist church, but that day I certainly did.

When Pastor Norman got back in the pulpit he made the statement that something great had just happened. He looked at me and asked if I would like to say anything. I responded, "Sure." That was very much out of character for me. I am the silent type. I went to the pulpit almost in a gallop and gazed out over the sea of faces that I did not know. I paused for a brief moment and said, "I knew none of you when I came in this church today, but at this moment I feel as if I have known all of you all of my life. I don't know what has happened to me, but I sure do like it." I returned to my seat as the pastor stated I had been saved. The congregation began to applaud and a statement was made that the angels in heaven were rejoicing. I didn't understand that statement either but by now it didn't matter.

Church was dismissed. Wally came to me and said, "You have been saved. You are now born again." I can say now that at that moment in the twinkling of the eye I became a child of the most-high God, a Christian, a believer; I was saved. The journey began.

I called Jane in Savannah and told her of my experience with Jesus. She, having been raised in church, knew exactly what I was talking about. She wept as we celebrated together. She and the children returned home not many days later and a new life in the Tuten house began to take shape. We were in church every time the doors opened, never missing a service or a function. We were soon involved in the choir, the youth program, and Sunday School. I couldn't get enough. It wasn't long until we were spending more time at church or in church activities than we were at home with each other. I didn't know at the time about church activities making tired saints.

On Wednesday evenings, we had a teaching service in which the pastor would expound on certain scriptures. I would sit and listen, but through no fault of the pastor, most of what he was saying was completely foreign to me. I was totally Bible illiterate. I had no reference points and no way of organizing in my mind the events or individuals he would discuss during his teaching or preaching sessions. I honestly thought his reference to Matthew, Mark, Luke, and John was to some friends of his. I did not know they were the first four books of the New Testament. I began to understand more by asking Jane questions and reading the scriptures for myself.

About a year later we were in Wednesday night service, sitting near the front of the church because I didn't want to miss one word being spoken. Suddenly God spoke to me, "I HAVE KEPT MY COVENANT WITH YOU, NOW KEEP YOUR COVENANT WITH ME, GIVE ME YOUR CIGARETTES." I was startled by the voice but knew who it was this time. I was a lover of cigarettes. I enjoyed smoking and would smoke three packs a day. I would awaken at night, prop my head on my hand and smoke. At times I would be so sleepy I could hardly stay awake.

By God's grace I never went to sleep with one in my hand. Most people would say one doesn't smoke that much; they just allow the cigarettes to burn up in the ashtray. The majority of mine were inhaled straight into the lungs with never one thought of how it looked, what it was doing to me or whom it was affecting. Apparently God did not want me smoking and instructed me to give them up.

I immediately got up while the pastor was still teaching, took the pack of Lucky Strikes and the lighter out of my shirt pocket, and walked to the rear of the church where Gladys Cox was sitting. I handed her the cigarettes and the lighter and said, "Please take these. God said to give them up." She took the pack and the lighter. She smiled and said nothing. I returned to my seat. All of this transpired without disturbing the teaching session in a matter of seconds. Little did I know that God was about to send me on the first journey of testing and faith I would experience.

The next day I began craving my cigarettes. I would reach to my shirt pocket for a cigarette and the pocket would be empty. I would remember what happened in church the night before and would try to push the burning desire aside. It would help for a moment then come back. I finally went to the Christian Bookstore in Cartersville and purchased a pocket Bible. I placed the Bible in my shirt pocket, and each time I would reach for the pack of cigarettes I would pull out the Bible. That helped to remind me of the words spoken by God a few days earlier.

Several days passed and I began to develop dizziness. I went to the doctor and his diagnosis was vertigo. He prescribed some medication, and I immediately began taking the medication because the dizziness was rapidly getting worse. A couple of days later the dizziness got so bad I couldn't drive, couldn't get to work, and the simple task of walking was a challenge at best. I finally had to lie on the couch. It seemed my head was spinning on my shoulders. I kept waiting for the medication to take affect, but the symptoms continued to worsen.

I began going to doctors, seeking the cause of my problem, because I was totally incapable of doing anything for myself. Several weeks passed, and the craving had subsided somewhat, but it was still there. The dizziness continued to be a severe problem. My family physician in Cartersville sent me to a neurologist in Rome, Georgia. Upon arrival the nurse took my vital signs, walked out of the office, and there Jane and I sat. I was in bad shape. I could barely hold my head up. Finally the doctor came in and took my blood pressure again. He said, "Mr. Tuten, your blood pressure is above stroke level, and I cannot dismiss you to go home. Mrs. Tuten, I have made arrangements for him to be admitted to the cardiac care center in Redmond Park Hospital. I don't know what is wrong with him, but all signs indicate a pending heart attack."

We left his office and reported to Redmond Park Hospital. They took me immediately to the cardiac care unit and began attaching all types and lengths of wire to my body. They instructed me to lie still and flat all the time giving me medication. Shortly after they completed their jobs the doctor came into the room. The doctor wasn't sure what was going on, but he wanted to observe me for at least 24 hours. I had no choice at this point but to consent since I was practically wired to the bed. The next afternoon the doctor returned to my room and stated my blood pressure had responded to the medication and had almost returned to normal. He said my heart was very stable. He wanted to know if I had changed anything in my normal routine of living. I told him I had stopped smoking. I had "cold-turkeyed" from three packs of cigarettes a day to nothing. He asked how long ago, and I told him several weeks. He said, "That's your problem. If you will smoke a cigarette all of these symptoms will go away. Do you want one?" I replied, "Absolutely not. You doctors are always saying to 'stop smoking' and now here I am trying to stop and you are asking me to smoke. No sir, I do not want a cigarette." The doctor replied, "There is nothing more we can do for you. You may go home. The problem is you smoked so much for so long your entire body is responding to the lack of nicotine. Your blood vessels are constricting causing the blood pressure to be elevated and that is reducing the blood flow to the brain causing the dizziness. Until your body adjusts to the lack of nicotine, these withdrawals, which is my diagnosis of your problem, will continue."

I left the hospital still very dizzy and disgusted. I had been out of work for weeks and was getting frustrated with myself and with my physical condition. I kept hearing the doctor's words, "Smoke a cigarette and you will be fine." I knew I couldn't. It was as though a cigarette in my mouth would violate my covenant with God. "Surely I would burn in hell," I thought. I refused to give in to the cravings, the symptoms, and the doctor.

Time continued to march forward and now five weeks had passed. I called my family doctor and talked with him again. This time I told him about the doctor in Rome and his comment. He said, "Ed, if you can hold on for eight weeks from the time you stopped smoking you will be fine." Now I had hope. Now I had something to grasp onto. My supervisor at work was very understanding and they continued to pay me the entire time I was out of work. I counted the days for the eight weeks to end. My entire day still consisted of bed to couch, couch to bed, as the dizziness did not cease.

The eight weeks ended on a Thursday. I waited with great expectation praying I would be fine. On Thursday morning I woke up and very slowly turned to get out of bed. This was the day of reckoning, the day I had been looking forward to in believing exactly what the doctor said, down to the day. As I slowly stood to my feet my balance was good, my legs were steady, and the dizziness was completely gone. Praise God in the highest!!! I returned to work that day and was glad to be there.

My addiction was broken, and I felt as if I had accomplished something. I was proud of myself. I had been able to do what God said to do. I learned from this experience to absolutely hate tobacco. There was never again a desire to smoke or get involved with any smoking or tobacco product. The smell of tobacco smoke sickens me, and I wonder now how I ever put one of those things in my mouth. I know me well. Had God graced me with a simple immediate deliverance I would probably at some time in the future have yielded to the temptation of tobacco and never been completely delivered. I passed the test not realizing that life in the future would be nothing but a series of tests… after test…after test…

Chapter 3
Learning To Trust

In April 1976, my family and I began attending the Cartersville Church of God. We were growing spiritually but had a great deal to learn, especially about the Holy Spirit. Shortly after we began attending services at the Cartersville Church of God, Jane received the Baptism in the Holy Spirit. My daughter Denise also received the Baptism in the Holy Spirit that summer during the Church of God camp meeting. My experience in receiving the Baptism in the Holy Spirit was more difficult. I had a very tough time receiving because I couldn't get "me" out of the way. I spent many months seeking this experience as well as an answer to what God's calling was on my life.

Finally, on Thanksgiving Eve 1976, in my living room, the Spirit of God flooded my soul as I prayed for Jane to receive healing in her back. The experience felt like Jesus had poured buckets of warm oil over my entire body. His presence was so real in my home that night it seemed I could literally reach out and touch Him. The manifestation of a heavenly language was evident for an hour or more. The scripture *with joy unspeakable and full of glory* (1Peter2:8b) became a beacon that night as the joy of the LORD filled my soul.

The next day, Thanksgiving Day, satan tried to make me doubt the experience I had the night before. We traditionally began decorating the Christmas tree on Thanksgiving. While Jane was preparing our meal, I was kneeling down at the front windows assembling the tree stand. I was thinking about the night before and the power that came through those same windows. At the same time, doubts were trying to creep in telling me it was all emotion and wasn't real. At that moment, the windows of heaven opened and the exact experience I had encountered the night before was repeated. The buckets of warm oil flooded my soul and from my innermost being came rivers of living water. This went on for about an hour. This time the children witnessed it.

When dinner was ready, the four of us sat down to eat. I usually said the blessing. We bowed our heads. Holding hands, I proceeded to bless the food. When I open my mouth to thank God for His many blessings, His love and mercy to us, and His bountiful grace, I again began speaking in a heavenly language that was uncontrollable. I could not speak in English so I just let it flow, allowing the Holy Spirit of God to bless our Thanksgiving dinner. I know God received our heartfelt thanks that day. It was directly from our hearts to His.

On my way to work early one January morning of 1977, I pulled into the first parking place on the north side of the new administration building and parked in my assigned space. Being excited as usual to report to work, I took my first step toward the front of the building, and suddenly out of complete silence with no one around, these words resounded in my head, "IS THIS WHAT YOU WANT TO DO THE REST OF YOUR LIFE?" Before my thought process could form a response, I immediately replied, "No!" Somewhat stunned I proceeded to work as usual. All through the day I could hear that question and my response. Being only three years old in the Lord, I wasn't really sure if what I had heard was Him or just my own thoughts. When I got home in the afternoon I shared with Jane what had happened but we never really understood or pursued counsel regarding the incident.

As time progressed the incident faded, and I didn't think much about what had happened.

Time continued to march onward. I began to notice I wasn't as happy about my job as in previous times. Feelings began to develop that were totally uncharacteristic of me or the way I felt about the job. I thought most of the unhappiness was my emotions. I would try to ignore these feelings and continue working as if nothing was wrong. Weekends would come, and rather than being excited about Monday to start back to work, I began dreading it. These feelings of dread and discontent grew worse as days and weeks passed. After a period of time I literally began to hate the job. I had lost all the peace and joy I had received in my salvation experience and the experience of the Holy Spirit Baptism a few months prior. I was absolutely miserable and didn't really have an answer as to why. I would pray, but the walls were as ping-pong paddles bouncing my words directly back to me. I was frustrated. My job performance was suffering and I knew it. There was nothing I could do about it as the discontent continued to grow. The most amazing thing was nothing had happened at work to cause me to be this miserable. My relationship with management and all the employees had not changed. My working conditions were the same. My job requirements were the same. Nothing changed. I would talk to Jane and we would pray, but were not getting any answers. We would discuss the situation, but no solution was evident, primarily because nothing was obviously wrong. Nothing was different.

I was making a good salary and our family was very happy. I still had to deal with the new feelings of discontent, and they were beginning to surface. My income was at a level that Jane didn't have to work and was able to stay at home with the children. Having her home to care for our children in their formative years was something we strongly desired even if it required me to work two or more jobs. When they started school we agreed she would work, but she would try to be home when they arrived from school. I was not frugal with our money and had the attitude to enjoy it while we could. There was no savings account. The checking account was always at a point with just enough money to keep it open. I didn't really worry about finances because I knew my job was very secure. I was never really taught to manage money so I was very carefree. We bought about anything we needed or wanted. If the money weren't readily available we would use credit cards. We had several of those in our possession and used them rather loosely. We always used the excuse that we could get it paid off in a few months, which of course we never did. This was our way of rationalizing and defending ourselves. We felt we deserved whatever we were buying at the time.

The thought began creeping into my mind to quit my job. I could always find another. I felt I had a fairly good resume and by this time was pretty confident of my abilities. The thoughts would sound something like this, "Why continue working at a job you literally hate? Quit." I didn't dare discuss these thoughts with Jane because I didn't want her to panic. My dislike for the job had become so intense and the desire to quit so overwhelming. One morning I had reached my wit's end. Finally, in early March without any thought or premeditated idea, I left the computer room, went upstairs to my supervisor's office, and asked if I could see him. He was very cordial and invited me in immediately. I went into his office, closed the door, and began talking to him. I stated I had become very disgruntled with the job. My dissatisfaction was not the fault of anyone or anything. I was unhappy. I said since I was unable to give him 100%, I simply could not continue working. He was very concerned because I did not have another job waiting for me. He stated it was much easier to find a job when you had one than to find one when you didn't. He asked if I would stay until the inventory was finished which was about six weeks away. I told him I would because it was a very involved process. I was the only employee in the company who had enough knowledge of the inventory computer system to properly use the computer for the inventory process. He asked me to train someone for the next inventory and see that all went well in the one coming up. I agreed and left his office.

When I reached the stairs to go back to my office the Holy Spirit of the Living God flooded me from the top of my head to the souls of my feet. The joy of the Lord consumed me. From my belly began flowing rivers of living water. I had not experienced that for many months. A heavenly language was pouring over my lips as water over Niagara Falls. I could feel the praises going from my inner most being straight to the Throne Room of God. It was as if the Lord and I had suddenly locked into each other. The walls, which prohibited my prayers from leaving the room, were totally gone. The channel of communication between my Father and me were opened and virtually all of me was going up to the Father and returning glorified. At least it felt that way especially since my walk with God was so new and young. I was reminded of Jacob's Ladder and the angels going up and down from earth to heaven. I returned to my desk, unable to stop my prayer language and the exhilaration I was feeling. The gentleman next to me in my office was not born again and had absolutely no idea what was happening. After a few minutes he left the office. He went to the keypunch area across the hall and told some of them what was happening to me the best he could. A few of them attended full-gospel churches and knew about the Baptism of the Holy Ghost. They suggested to him that I be left alone. Several hours passed before reality returned to me. That afternoon when I got home I asked Jane to have a seat and listen to me a minute. I told her as best I could what had happened that day concerning my joy returning and the exhilaration I felt then and was still feeling. I shared with her I had turned in my notice at work and the inventory completion would be my last day. She was as happy as I was that my joy had returned. I am positive she was tired of me griping about the job; however, all of that would soon end. We talked a few minutes, and I assured her as best I could that all would be okay. She seemed comforted and at peace. I truly believe God had already prepared her heart.

The remainder of my stay at the mill through inventory was pleasurable. I didn't have the bitter hatred anymore and the last few weeks were enjoyable. God had worked a miracle in restoring my joy, and for that I was grateful, but I was still ready to leave. Finally, the last day had arrived. It was Good Friday, April 15, 1977. I left the mill for the last time. I had in my possession my current week's pay, plus two weeks vacation pay. I left with no malice against anyone, but I knew I didn't ever want to work there again. God had seen to that in a very profound way.

I arrived home and told Jane it was over. I felt very relieved, happy, and so full of the Lord. The fact I didn't have a job now didn't trouble me one minute. I explained to Jane I had my regular week's pay plus two weeks of vacation pay. I also explained to her this was all the money we had. Jane at the time was babysitting the young boy next door. The mother was paying her $20 a week. I soon realized that was all the income we would have until I found another job.

The next Sunday was Easter. Jane, the children, and I went to church as usual. The four of us did a little singing at the time and the Lord had quickened Jane to ask the pastor if we could sing, *The Three Nails* during the Easter service. He stated the morning was already filled with special music and would we mind singing in the evening service. The song was about the crucifixion and the nails that were used. The song described the place where the nails were purchased and the merchant who sold them. My part in the song was speaking the narration after the three of us sang a verse. That Easter Sunday evening service we were standing on the platform preparing to sing. Everyone else including the pastor was sitting in the congregation. Jane, Denise, and I sang the first verse. As I began the narration while they hummed a verse, I heard the word, "PREACH." I was startled because the voice was male sounding. I took a quick look to be sure the pastor had not come to the platform without my knowledge, and he hadn't. All the time I am still reciting the narrative, without interruption, trying to figure out where the voice came from. As I reached the last line of the narrative I heard it again, the same tone and the same voice. It said, "PREACH." By this time the song was over, and we quickly made our way back to our seats. I was still at a loss about what and whom I heard.

We had to downsize our living standards tremendously from what we were accustomed. We had a house payment of $180 a month, a number of credit cards with fairly large balances, and the usual utility bills. Of course there was also the grocery bill and needs for the children's education. The paychecks that I received upon leaving the mill were soon exhausted. I paid all the bills I could, leaving enough money to keep the checking account open.

I began job hunting. I filed applications everywhere I could find. I checked with the labor department. I watched the newspaper. I went to Savannah where I was raised. I searched. There was not a job to be found. I was willing to take anything, and I would tell this to prospective employers, but they would not hire me. According to them, I was either over-qualified or under-qualified for the particular opening that was available. The situation at home was getting, at least in my eyes, desperate. On one particular occasion I read an ad in the help wanted section of the newspaper. I got dressed and drove to the address on South Tennessee Street. I stopped the car in front of the building and cut the engine off. The Lord spoke to me as clearly as if a human was in the car, "THIS JOB IS FILLED." I said in a very disgusted manner, "We'll see." I started the car and returned home, which was only three minutes away. I admit I was somewhat irritated. I picked up the same newspaper in which I had seen the article and proceeded to call the business. When the receptionist answered the phone, I asked about the particular job for which I was going to apply. Her immediate comment was, "That job is taken, but thank you for calling." I was astounded. I finally began to put two-and-two together and realized that this whole thing was not under my control but His and His alone. The voice I was hearing was not my imagination but the voice of God.

I filed approximately 40 applications in the city of Cartersville. At that time Cartersville was a very small town by any standard. This number did not include the applications filed in other towns and cities. There was not a job anywhere. It seemed as if I was incapable of working anywhere but a carpet mill. There is nothing wrong with working in a carpet mill, but by now I hated the smell in the air that was produced by the different mills as they manufactured carpet. God had completely turned around my desire to do anything but follow Him, although at the time I was not aware what was happening.

All of our money was gone. Only by the grace of God was the babysitting money of $20 a week still coming in. This did allow us to get a few staple items to put food in the kitchen cabinets. By now the cabinets were practically empty. We would purchase items that would last such as bags of dried beans, potatoes, rice, etc. I spent a number of days in serious prayer. Being new in the Lord there was a great deal of confusion and frustration on my part. The frustration and confusion were the result of my thinking process. I would have thoughts such as, "Why is God allowing this to happen to us? We have committed our lives to Him. Why can't I find a job? Am I so unqualified to work anywhere that nobody wants me as their employee? Has God forsaken me? Did I really hear God that morning in the parking lot? Was it God that took the desire from me to continue working at the mill?

What is really going on?" It would concern me because I felt as if my family was suffering from the lack of things and events to which we were accustomed. Food and money was becoming a precious commodity. I was supposed to be the provider for my wife and two small children. Becoming very distraught, I began to entertain thoughts of being a complete failure and totally worthless as a husband, a father, and a man.

Only a few weeks had passed since leaving my job, but it seemed like months. I was unable to collect unemployment because I had voluntarily quit my job with no adverse reason for doing so except I hated it. I knew what the Bible said about men not caring for their own household. I also knew it said to trust God. I did not know how to trust something or someone I could not see or deal with on a personal, verbal, one-on-one basis. The "not caring for" scripture was really grinding in my soul. I was miserable. Nothing seemed to be accomplished by praying. I wasn't even sure I knew how to pray or whether God was even listening. My feeble efforts at praying seemed to go nowhere and accomplish nothing.

I spent many hours on my face trying to find answers. "What was wrong with me? What had I done wrong to deserve this harsh treatment? Had I let God down with my inability to support my family? Was God mad at me? What does God want me to do now and for the remainder of my life?" All of these thoughts and more raced through my head in an endless circle of repetition. The harder and longer I prayed it seemed the fewer answers I got. I wept. I got aggravated. I would sit and stare for hours with a completely blank mind hoping somehow God would overlook my perceived shortcomings and speak something to me I understood. Hours turned into days. Days turned into weeks with little or no change.

One night while my family and I were sleeping a very disturbing incident took place. All my life everyone called me Eddie. On this particular night we were sleeping soundly, and as always, Jane and I kept a window in the bedroom opened slightly to get fresh air, plus I liked the coolness on my face.

About 2 a.m. I was awakened by the sound of someone calling my name. "EDDIE...EDDIE...EDDIE," I heard as the twilight of the half asleep, half awake state began to overtake me. As I became more alert I immediately assumed one of our relatives had driven from Savannah to spend some time with us. I thought that it might be Jane's dad calling to me through the slightly opened window since the doors were all locked. I sat up and turned to get out of bed in order to let him in. As my feet touched the floor I heard these words, "SPREAD THE GOSPEL AROUND THE WORLD," spoken as clearly as if someone had been standing in the room speaking directly to me. I immediately recognized what had happened and who had spoken. I was so shaken I proceeded to the kitchen, grabbed a jar of peanut butter, and began eating. I was a nervous wreck, and I don't think I slept the remainder of the night. The next morning I told Jane what had happened and we both began trying to figure out what was spoken and why. What in the world was going on?

The next night, still somewhat on edge from the previous night, the same thing happened about the same time of the morning. At around 2 a.m. I heard, "EDDIE...EDDIE." This time I was ready and immediately turned to get up. When I did these words resounded in my ears, "PREACH THE HOLY GHOST." I awoke Jane and said, "It happened again." I shared with her the best I could of what I heard. Neither of us still had any understanding of the meaning. We knew what was said, but I wanted to know what was meant. I again was physically and emotionally shaken.

A few days afterward I presented the happenings of those two nights to my pastor. He said, "That's what God wants you to do, spread the gospel around the world." I said, "Jesus gave all of us that instruction in His word." He said, "But He has spoken specifically to you and has given you personally that command." "How am I supposed to do that?" I answered. He stated, "When God is ready, He will let you know; I wouldn't worry about it if I were you."

Not long after leaving my job in April I realized I had a bank draft for life insurance amounting to $50 coming out of my checking account at the bank on the 15th of May and each month thereafter. I had about two dollars in the account. In a near panic I told Jane the situation and she in her beautiful way of calming me down said, "God will take care of us." This concept was completely foreign to me. After all, a man was supposed to be the breadwinner for his family. It was the man's job and his alone. Anything other than that was totally unacceptable.

The 15th was rapidly approaching. It was the Sunday before the bank draft was due to be deducted from our account and we were preparing for church as usual. Fifty dollars to cover the bank draft may as well have been a million dollars. The Lord let it be known to Jane that our attitude toward Him was very important at all times. This made me feel I was being hypocritical. I was down emotionally because of our circumstances, but we

41

evidently were to act as if nothing was wrong and that our situation, including finances, was fine. Jane had an outgoing, upbeat personality and was always in a good mood. She wasn't nearly as concerned about our circumstances as I was. She could show her true feelings, and it wouldn't be a lie. I, on the other hand, do not hide my feelings well. For me to present a happy, joyful attitude is extremely difficult. Worry, disgust, and any other adverse emotions readily show on my face. In order to be obedient I tried to be "happy," but I knew my torn emotions were evident.

I felt as if my face and actions were a chalkboard of information about our situation and us. No one ever said anything. I was positive my feelings were on display in front of the entire congregation or anyone else with which I came in contact. Jane having been raised in church knew more about God than I. She had an uncanny peace about her that I simply could not grasp. As we walked into church Sunday morning before that fateful date of May 15, Jane began inviting ladies to our home for a Tuesday night prayer meeting. I was in full agreement with that because I definitely needed prayer, not only for our situation, but my attitude concerning how I felt about myself and toward God.

As Tuesday evening arrived the individuals Jane had invited began arriving as planned for the prayer meeting. Upon arriving, each had a bag of groceries in their arms. When I saw what was happening an attitude of pure pride began to swell up in me. I was totally embarrassed. I felt like they thought we asked them to pray at our home rather than going to one of theirs so they could see our depraved situation and maybe bring some food or money to help. I was devastated. The third and then the fourth person came in. All had bags of food. I, although quiet, was by now nearly a basket case. Jane looked at me smiling in her usual jovial manner, read the look on my face concerning what was happening, turned and said, "If I had known you were going to do this I would have asked you to come sooner." There was a complete meltdown of the tension on my part as they began to laugh. Laughter and neck hugging was now the order of the day. In a matter of a few moments with a comment from a Godly woman my whole attitude for the evening had changed.

The prayer meeting went as planned. It began to break up about 9 p.m. When all of the prayer warriors left we began unloading the groceries. Our cupboards and refrigerator were practically bare, because there was no money to buy food. As I removed the groceries from the bags passing them to Jane to put in the cabinets, we noticed that all items were the same brands that we used when times were better and we could afford to buy groceries. When I got to the bottom of the bag there was an envelope. I removed it and opened it to find a card with a written prayer concerning God's blessings to fill our home. Inside the card was a $5 bill. I began unloading another bag of groceries and at the bottom of that bag was a card and another $5 bill. I unloaded another bag. At the bottom of the bag there was another card. I opened the card. It had scripture to sustain and lift us up. Inside that card was a $10 bill. This scenario repeated itself time after time, bag after bag. When all the bags were emptied and put away, I counted the money and there was a grand total of $45. The disgust and frustration began to arise in me, and being the sarcastic one that I can be at times, I made this comment, "Well

God you missed it this time. I needed $50 and you only sent $45."

I immediately took on the attitude that God tried but failed, and I was still going to lose my insurance policy because the draft would be returned due to insufficient funds. Jane chided me for my rotten attitude but that didn't help matters. I was still angry. We decided to go bed. I reached to turn off the kitchen lights and noticed another bag of groceries in the corner that neither of us had seen. We didn't see anyone bring it in nor did either of us put it there. I proceeded to give each grocery item to Jane. When I unloaded the last of the items there was an envelope in the bottom of that bag. I took the envelope, opened it and read the front of the card. When I proceeded to read the inside, lying in the fold of the card was a $50 bill. I absolutely melted in shame. I fell on my face in our shag carpet floor trying to pull the fibers apart, because I couldn't get low enough to humble myself before a God that went to a lot of trouble to show little insignificant me that He is here, and He would meet all of our needs.

All of my ugliness did not circumvent the purpose, which He had divinely ordained that evening to accomplish. I had to learn to trust Him. I must have lain in the floor for well over one hour asking for forgiveness, shedding pride, and knocking off some attitudes that were not Holy in His sight. How could a God so loving and faithful forgive my rotten stinking attitude, not to mention being totally disrespectful? I finally got up off the floor and went to bed still feeling pretty bad at my attitude, but somehow knew that all was okay between God and myself. I got up the next morning, went to the bank, and deposited the $95 that God had supplied the night before. The draft was covered and there was enough money to pay a few more bills. Our cabinets were filled with God's supply of our brand of foods, not to mention the refrigerator being well stocked. I had also learned a lesson about God's mercy. I had received favor and definitely did not deserve it. That event was, and remains to this day, a lesson in God's grace, love, and mercy.

That was truly the first miraculous showing of God's hand during five months without employment, $20 a week income, no health insurance, and no money for the necessities of life. We had no choice but to continue life no matter how dark the time seemed.

Summer was fast approaching, and I was preparing myself psychologically to endure the hot and humid north Georgia summer without our air conditioning. The summers are almost unbearable, adding to the fact I am very hot natured. My dress for the winter was generally short-sleeved shirts and occasionally a jacket on the very coldest days. One day the Lord spoke to me, "DO NOT TURN YOUR AIR CONDITIONING OFF." Jane and I had already discussed turning the A/C off and had reconciled ourselves to the fact that we would need to go without the A/C to conserve money. I told Jane what God had just spoken. We concluded He was obviously going to somehow pay the power bill since we were total electric. I knew with my income, which was nothing, and with her income of $20 a week, we would not be able to pay the power bill. We decided at this point we were going to accept Him at His Word and see what happened. I had read in the Bible to try God. He had spoken. Now we were going to stand on that Word.

There was a lot of pride that had to be broken from us. Jane and I would pray asking God to send us some help. When it came in the form of a "hand-out" we would say, "Oh no, we are fine," after just asking God for help. We would receive money at church, on the street, in a store, at home, and even through the mail. Individuals would give Jane or myself money saying, "God said to give this to you." Pride quickly became a non-issue. We would go to the car for a trip to town or church and there would be an envelope under the windshield wiper containing money. There would be times when we would open the front door of the house and there would be an envelope under a rock on the front stoop containing money. On one occasion, Denise opened the door to go to the mailbox. On the carport were two sacks of groceries and there was no one around that could have left them. Our cabinets were getting bare and God knew it. Money or food was never there unless it was needed. We learned to stretch a dollar and live meagerly, even doing without things we thought were necessities and finding they were luxuries. One day while at the drugstore the children asked for a candy bar. There wasn't enough money with all of us to buy one, not to mention two pieces of candy. You can only imagine how I felt. I told them I was sorry but maybe God would give them their desire at a later date.

The bills including credit card payments, utilities, and the house payments were continuing to stack up in our "unpaid bill" holder. I didn't worry about them because I couldn't pay them and all the contributions people were so generously giving us, and Jane's babysitting money didn't amount to enough to pay them all or even get them current. I called and tried to explain to creditors but they didn't understand. My home was mortgaged through Cartersville Federal Savings and Loan in Cartersville. I talked to them. They listened to me and understood my plight. They stated they would work with me as long as I kept them posted on my job situation. They would temporarily suspend the payment on the principle but the interest would continue to accrue. The plan as developed was when I secured a job I would pay a specified amount based on the pay rate each pay period until the interest was current. That was very satisfactory, especially since I didn't have a job and wasn't in a position to bargain. I felt they were being more than fair to me, and I certainly appreciated it. That solution did not however solve my numerous credit card and other bill problems. We were getting calls from the creditors daily wanting to know when they could expect payment. It was very frustrating and embarrassing, but there was absolutely nothing I could do. Jane and I made it a point not to share our plight with other people and desperately tried to maintain the good attitude that God had instructed soon after I quit work.

As time drifted on I continued to seek employment but to no avail. All the doors were shut, and man was not going to open them until God was ready. By this time it was general knowledge through the church and our friends that I was unemployed, but our attitude did remain positive. At least Jane's did all the time and mine most of the time. It was getting easier to do.

One evening, Jane was babysitting for some friends while I remained home with our children. About 9 p.m. that evening, Johnnie Graves called Jane at the friend's house and said, "Jane, I can't get you, those children, and Ed off my mind. I have thought about it all day, and God

47

will not turn me loose. I can't sleep and I can't eat. In the morning I am coming to your house, and I want you to give me all your bills." Jane not understanding began to ask questions. Johnnie said, "Please don't ask any questions, because I can't tell you anything." Jane told Johnnie she would give them to her but she would have to talk to me first. The next morning Johnnie was at our house to gather our bills. Jane had already told me what was happening, and we were both in the dark as to what was going on. Johnnie again said, "Please don't ask any questions, because I can't tell you." She turned to me and said, "Ed, give me all your bills and your house payment book." I knew Johnnie well enough to know if she said God was dealing with her then He was. I gathered all of the bills and the payment book as she requested and put them in a paper sack. Very puzzled by this entire ordeal, I gave her what she requested. She took the bag filled with unpaid bills and left the house leaving a lot of unanswered questions.

In about a week Johnnie returned to our home bringing with her another of God's wondrous miracles. She asked if we could sit and talk. Jane and I sat with her at our dining room table. She handed me my house payment book and some receipts and said, "All of your bills are caught up with the exception of your house payment. Please don't ask any questions, because I can only tell you that God gave me names of people to visit to ask for contributions to pay off your bills. They are to forever remain a secret to you. Please don't ask, because I can't tell you."

Jane and I were flabbergasted and began to weep almost uncontrollably. There was complete and total shock. I could not understand why anyone would want to hand out hard earned money to pay off another person's debts that were created out of a lack of wisdom. Why would someone give money to pay the bills of someone they hardly knew? Johnnie asked that we cut up all of our credit cards stating we needed to learn to get along without them. I took a pair of scissors and cut them into a thousand pieces. The emotional relief of this wondrous work of God's Hand in getting these bills current was overwhelming. There was tremendous relief from the stress of many past due bills, many phone calls, and no money. Since all the bills were now current as a result of Johnnie Graves' obedience, the bill collectors stopped calling. For a short period of time it seemed this trial we were experiencing was coming to an end.

After a while I noticed the remaining bills such as utilities, phone, and the normal monthly bills were beginning to get behind and money wasn't as forthcoming as before. Individuals were not as free with their assistance, and we didn't understand why. We began fervently praying about the situation seeking God for reasons. I had learned to seek God for answers to problems, and this was evolving into a major problem again. His immediate reply to me was, "YOU ARE DEPENDING ON PEOPLE AND NOT ME."

In searching my heart, I could readily see my trust was being placed in the resources of man and not the storehouse of God. I along with Jane began praying that our dependency would turn to Him again and we would have the wisdom to know how to fully trust God and not man. We did not want our trust to be in individuals even though they were the ones He was using to fulfill His will and purpose.

49

It is extremely difficult not to depend on the source you actually see meeting your need. Learning to put your trust in a Deity that can't be seen requires a great deal more faith than I felt I had. We prayed...and we prayed...and we prayed almost without ceasing for the problem of trusting God and not man, plus the entire unemployment situation.

Money wasn't available for anything. My ego was completely shattered, and my pride was a thing of the past. I needed to talk to someone. I needed counsel. Jane called Fred and Pat Harris to see if we could visit and just fellowship for a while. They invited us to their home and as always they were very receptive and hospitable. We talked and shared about the Lord, the beauty of His Word, and the promises He put forth in the Word. They knew I was unemployed, but I don't believe they knew our real circumstances. The subject about being jobless was never mentioned. We stayed a short while not wanting to wear out our welcome. The fellowship was good for Jane as it was for me. As we moved into the front yard to leave, Fred and Pat were standing in the front doorway. He called to me and said, "Ed, remember the Word says, *I have not seen the righteous forsaken, nor His seed begging bread*"(Psalms 37:25b). Those words pierced me like a knife. Suddenly a promise, a word for which I had been searching came forth from the lips of his servant. These words gave me hope. The Lord wasn't going to forsake us or let us go hungry no matter what the circumstances seemed. Those words gave me something to hold to until God completed what He was trying to do. They gave me faith to believe Him for a timely ending to all of this. I can still hear those words today resounding from Fred as if God himself had spoken them. Somehow

God did speak those words and the Spirit of the Living God used them to comfort my soul and give me peace.

The time was now approaching late summer. School opening was around the corner. Jane and I both knew that there was no money for clothes or supplies. The first day of school was on Thursday and they were off on Friday. When Denise and Howard returned home on Thursday each had a list seemingly a mile long of things they needed for school. It may as well have been a request to purchase Hoover Dam. Jane and I prayed concerning this need and many others that had accumulated during the months since Johnnie had completed her step of obedience. How was God going to supply this? Would He supply it now that our trust had been put in man? I was deeply concerned because I knew if the children didn't have the supplies by the first part of the week they would not only be humiliated and embarrassed, but would probably be sent home from school.

The next morning was Saturday. Denise and Howard were out of bed. Jane and I were awake and getting up. Denise opened the door to go to the mailbox. There on the carport were five paper bags. She said, "Daddy, what is this?" I went to the door, picked up the bags, and brought them inside. I looked to see if anyone was around, and I saw a vehicle going to the other end of the street, but I could not identify it. Inside the bags were the school supplies needed for Denise and Howard. Each had two sacks with their supplies in them: everything the school had requested and a little more. The children were excited because they would be able to go to school and not concern themselves with not having the proper supplies. The fifth bag contained much needed groceries.

Jane and I were elated because God had once more shown He was in control and our sole supplier. We wept realizing He had heard our prayers concerning the trust issue. We thanked Him over and over for the miracle He had performed for our children and us as well. He let the children know He cared for them as much as He did mom and dad, and He would also meet their need.

On another occasion, I was attending a church meeting. Jane and the children were home alone. Jane was sitting at the table reading the newspaper when there was a "thud" outside. It sounded like a rock had been thrown at the front door. Denise asked her mom, "What was that?" Jane told her she didn't know to go to the door and see. Denise opened the door and saw a car going down the road. There had been numerous paper bags placed on the front stoop. Bringing them inside, Jane discovered each bag was full of much needed groceries. All the items were the same brand names we used prior to me leaving work. It was another of God's miracles to teach us He did supply our need if we would only trust Him and not man. At a much later date, we found out who left the bags of groceries. The lady said to us, "God told her which items and what brands to purchase."

During the five months while out of work with just $20 a week to live and pay bills God taught me a great deal about Himself and myself. It was only in retrospect that I could see what He was doing during this time. I did notice however, I was no longer too proud to take a "hand-out," and I did have a lot more faith in God and who He was. I thought I served Him but realized that my service to the Lord was lip service and not heart service. It took more than going to church, reading my Bible, and praying. It took a commitment to believe He could under every circumstance meet our need, and we were to serve Him no matter the difficulty of the trial or situation being experienced. It wasn't left to man to determine or meet the need of my family. It was God's timing and resources that ultimately met our need. I realized my wife and children were gifts and not something I deserved.

During this time there was no sickness with any family member. Not one of us lost a pound of weight from lack of food. We never missed a meal. Our clothes and shoes remained wearable without looking tattered or torn. All bills were paid through God's supply with the exception of the house payment. Georgia Power was always paid. On one occasion someone paid a delinquent bill without our knowledge, allowing the power to remain on using the air conditioning all summer. My insurance policy was never cancelled because of a draft being missed. I am still deducting that draft 25 years later. We voluntarily placed our home on the market to sell for just what we owed. It never sold. There wasn't one inquiry concerning the sale of the house. God supplied that home originally, and His intent was for us to live in it and watch the salvation of our lives as His grace and mercy unfolded before our eyes.

Chapter 4
Learning How To Pray

I continued to search the newspapers for job opportunities, not looking for any particular type of job. I was searching for something that would provide income. I had long overcome the idea that employment had to be a job in my field of "expertise." On the evening of September 29, 1977, while reviewing the want ads, I saw a job opening for a night auditor at a motel on Interstate 75 at the Cass-White exit just north of Cartersville. I immediately related the word auditor with bookkeeping and felt I might qualify for this job. The next morning I got dressed in my usual interview clothes and went to the location. I inquired about the job and was asked to fill out an application. The manager would be with me shortly.

He soon came to where I was seated in the restaurant area of the motel complex and invited me to his office. To get to his office required a very long walk through the kitchen. Upon arrival in his office I was amazed anyone could work in such cramped space. His desk was just far enough away from the wall to get his chair into a position in which he could actually sit. There was no room to slide his chair back away from the desk to get out. If there had been arms on the chair he would have had to crawl over the arm to get from behind his desk. The chair in which I sat was practically against the front of the desk. There was barely enough room for my legs when sitting. The back of the chair was against the wall.

He looked over my application making a few favorable comments about my past experience. He explained to me the job was from 11 p.m. to 7 a.m. Sunday through Thursday. He said it required preparing accounting reports from each day's motel and gas business, renting rooms when tourists stopped during my shift, plus selling gas by turning on the pumps from the inside of the building and collecting money for the gas sold. The building would be locked, and except in extreme emergency, I was not to leave the inside of the building. He then said he would be interviewing a few others for the job but to call him about 2 p.m., and he would let me know whether or not the job was mine. It was a very short interview and pay was not even discussed at this time. Any pay was better than what I had, so it wasn't really an important issue.

As the interview came to a conclusion, I suddenly had an overwhelming feeling the job was mine. It was as if I knew there were no more interviews and I, for the first time in five months, had a job. My knees and hands began to tremble as the Spirit of God flooded my soul. My mouth went numb. I could hardly speak. My jerking knees were visibly bouncing up and down as I desperately tried to hold them still. All the time I thought, "What in the world is this man going to think. If he sees me, I know he will think I am having some type of seizure and there will go my newly found job." I quickly, but as politely as possible, ended the interview. I shook his hand across the desk with my trembling hand. He asked if I was okay. I assured him I was just a little nervous but fine. I stood to leave his office, and my head began to reel as if I was drunk. I could hardly stand. I gained my footing and began walking to my car. I first had to go through the long kitchen, make a left turn, and walk through the restaurant to the front door to get to my car. As I walked very slowly through the kitchen with my hand on the wall to balance myself, the kitchen personnel would politely smile and speak. I was trying my best to look and act normal, but by now I had developed tunnel vision and could only see straight ahead. I would nod acknowledging them the best I could while holding to the wall. As I reached the end of the kitchen making the turn to go through the dining room, I realized there was no wall on which to hold and I was on my own. I was obviously drunk in the Spirit. My legs were weak and trembling and my eyes had completely lost all peripheral vision. I was seeing straight ahead and straight ahead only.

Across the dining room near the front door was a cigarette machine. I held on to the wall and focused my eyes on the Lucky Strike cigarettes in that machine. I mustered the strength to move forward and turned loose of the wall. I was walking very slow and deliberate so as not to appear inebriated. As I passed a gentleman in the booth to my immediate left he said, "Hello." Without a thought I turned and said, "Hello." I lost my balance and began to stagger wildly, almost colliding with an empty table. I could not find the cigarette machine with the Lucky Strike cigarettes quick enough. I determined I had better get out of there in a hurry before I fell on my face or was seen by anyone that would tell the manager I was drunk. I started throwing one foot in front of the other and literally ran the remaining few feet out of the building.

Drunk in the Spirit and speaking in tongues, I got in the car and started driving. I had absolutely no concept of where I was or how to get home. I can't recall how long I drove. The next thing I knew I was in front of Dan River Carpet in White, Georgia. Recognizing the place I was able to navigate home without a great deal of added difficulty.

When I arrived home Jane was vacuuming and the TV was on The 700 Club. I walked in, and she immediately recognized the Spirit of God was upon me. I was still drunk from the new wine, speaking in a heavenly language and trembling all over. She turned the vacuum cleaner off. The 700 Club was about to broadcast the first live picture of the Eastern Gate in Jerusalem. As the countdown to that historic moment was taking place, I walked to the television and placed both of my hands on the screen. When the picture came into view I began to praise the Lord in my prayer language again. As I praised God, He gave the interpretation to Jane. I was saying, "Oh my Messiah, Oh my Messiah." For the next couple of hours I remained awash in the Holy Spirit of God.

I later shared with Jane I was sure the job was mine, but I had to call the manager at 2:00 p.m. At the two o'clock hour, I made the phone call hoping my apparent drunkenness had not been brought to his attention. He came to the phone and said, "The job is yours, when can you start work?" I said, "As soon as you need me." He replied, "Good, plan to start October 3. Come in an hour early so we can begin training."

On October 3, 1977, I arrived at my new job on time. I was very anxious to begin work for the first time since mid-April. It was at this time I learned my pay was $120 a week and payday was on Friday.

All went well, and I quickly learned my responsibilities and was able to be left alone. Upon receiving my first check, I went to Cartersville Federal Savings and Loan to complete the agreement we had made earlier in the year. It was decided that I would need to pay $75 a week until the interest was current. That didn't leave us much to live on, but it certainly was better than we had.

The job at the motel soon became a job I didn't like at all. Some of the traveling public, I quickly found out, were very rude, harsh, and had very distasteful dispositions. I tried to rationalize they had been traveling and were tired, but that didn't help my feelings any. I was not the confrontational type and would make every attempt to avoid arguments. Management would require all reservations cancelled if not confirmed or filled by 10 p.m. Tourists would arrive at eleven, midnight, and one o'clock in the morning expecting to occupy the room they had reserved, only to find it had been rented and nothing was available to suit their needs. They would go into a rage, cursing, screaming, yelling at me, calling me names, threatening, and any other demeaning tactic that a human could possibly exhibit. The only thing that kept me from being physically struck by someone a number of times was the plexiglas window between them and me. People would steal gas by driving off and not paying for it. Finally management decided to make people pay before pumping. This was another reason for some people to throw tantrums, curse, acting completely irrational and uncivilized. A number of times I thanked God I was locked inside the building, because I was sure if I had been exposed to the outside, I would have gotten hurt or possibly killed from the anger expressed by some of the customers patronizing that business.

Progressively my dislike for the job got so bad that as I crossed over the Interstate at Cass-White exit while going to work, I would look at the volume of cars riding the Interstate. I would say, "God, do not let there be many tourists tonight. Don't let them stop at the motel where I have to work." Each time someone would stop for gas or rent a room I would nearly panic from the fear of possible direct confrontation that could take place. On one particular occasion I was asked to come in early. It was an exceptionally busy night both in the restaurant and in the motel. A male traveler came in to rent a room he supposedly reserved. The reservation had not been received or it had been lost. It wasn't there and all rooms had been rented. It was about 9:30 in the evening. The person absolutely lost all control. He exploded with profanity and yelled at the top of his voice. In his rage he came behind the counter threatening to kill the female clerk who, at that particular time, was also the assistant manager. She turned to me and yelled, "Call the police." As she spoke those words a policeman came in the door. Upon seeing the policeman, the raged individual picked up a pencil and threw it directly at the clerk. The pencil missed her, bounced off the walls nearly striking me in the head as it came to rest on the desk by where I stood. The man left the premises with the parting comment, "You haven't heard the last of me." He got into his car and drove off.

The next several nights I lived in constant fear that he was a man of his word and would return. He never did. This type of incident and all of the nightly cursing out I would get for doing my job soon made me dread the thought of going to work even more than I did the night before. I would spend my time at home during the evening hours crying and praying. I was dreading every minute that passed before I had to leave at 10:30 p.m. During the quiet hours at work, usually about two or three in the morning, I would pray, "God, why did you give me such an ugly job where people were so inconsiderate of other people? Would you please find me another job?" After a while He let me know I had asked Him for "any job" so that is what He gave me. I quickly learned to be very specific in my prayer request. I began praying for a day job. I prayed for a job in which people at least would treat others with respect and not like a sub-servant to be stepped on like a dirty, filthy slug. I prayed for a job that would better supply my families needs primarily through a better wage.

One morning after arriving home from work, I was sitting in the lounging chair crying out to God. In the midst of this Jane was awakened from the sound of my lamenting. She knelt beside me and prayed. God showed her the job was only for a season. I wasn't sure how long God's seasons were, and my anguish over the job continued to worsen. I regretted every moment leading up to work time and every moment while working. My dislike was so bad that I would pull up into the parking area, cut the engine and the lights off, and sit there sometimes crying and always hating to open the car door to go into the job site. My emotions were in shambles, and I wasn't sure how much more of this abuse I could take.

The Christmas season was upon us. With the bills to be paid including the $75 a week to the Savings and Loan, we didn't have money for gifts for the children and none for other family members including Jane or myself. We explained to Denise and Howard this would be a very slim Christmas because we didn't have money to buy presents for anyone.

We had an artificial tree and many decorations had accumulated through the years. Jane and I decorated the house just as always in an effort to make Christmas as normal as possible for the children. I'll admit in years prior to this we probably went overboard with the festivities, presents, and the "Santa Claus" syndrome, but this year would have to be different. As Christmas Day approached with nothing under the tree, my heart was being eaten away. Christmas was always a big deal when I was growing up, and I had a lot of excellent memories. This is what I wanted for my children – heritage, a memory full of wonderful times with the family. That was my desire for them. During past Christmas seasons the emphasis was always placed on material things since we knew of no spiritual.

On Christmas Eve there was a knock at the front door and there stood a friend of ours. She and her sister had each bought a boy and girl gift. She handed them to me, and I put them under the tree. There were now a total of four gifts in our home. We thanked her, wished her a Merry Christmas, and she left.

That evening I read the Christmas story from the Bible, kissed and hugged the children good night, and all of us went to bed. Christmas morning arrived. We got up early as usual on Christmas Day. I went into the living room first, as I always did, and plugged in the tree lights. I looked around an empty living room completely void of toys and the usual number of gifts the kids would normally receive for Christmas. A large lump came into my throat as I fought the tears of disappointment I felt for Denise, Howard, and Jane. My heart was aching because I was unable to give my family Christmas. For a brief moment, I felt empty, and I felt as if I had failed my beautiful family with the emptiness of the living room that Christmas morning. I quickly tried to shake off those feelings and look at the spiritual side of Christmas for the first time.

Suddenly, I realized that my heavenly Father had supplied Christmas for us. It wasn't awash with materialism and fantasy but with the love that only God could give. All of this transpired in a few seconds time. I called Jane and the children into the living room and said, "Let's pray before we open the gifts our Heavenly Father sent to us." I prayed thanking God for His bountiful supply and showing us that Christmas is not giving and receiving presents, but Christmas is giving and receiving the love of God and the love of one another. I handed Denise her two gifts and Howard his two gifts. They opened them with thanksgiving in their hearts. Each of the gifts was something each had wanted but didn't ask for because they knew I couldn't afford to buy them. Both of them were just as happy with their two gifts as any child I saw that had received many times more but with less love.

Jane prepared dinner as usual on Christmas since we had no family in Cartersville. My sister and her family had moved to Missouri by this time. The four of us spent the most wonderful Christmas we had ever experienced together as the love of God continued to fill our home that day. "God, Four Gifts, and a Day," will always burn in Jane's and my heart as the most beautiful Christmas ever in the Tuten home. I learned a great deal from that experience. Christ is now and will forever more be the center of Christmas, as well as any other day of the year in our home.

One weekend in February 1978, while reading the want ads I saw an ad for a merchandising manager at Dunaway's Drug Store in Cartersville. I applied for the job and was immediately hired. I had to give a two-weeks notice at the motel to be fair to management there. After all, it wasn't their fault I was so miserable. It was my inability to handle the cursing, arguing, and feuding from the customers. The next evening as I reported for work at the motel the manager was waiting for me. He was usually gone when I arrived but that night was an exception.

He asked if we could talk in his office for a few minutes; he would let the second shift work over until we finished. We walked back to that same cramped office and were seated. He said, "Ed, I will get right to the point. I have been talking to the regional officials about you and we are very impressed with you and your work. We would like for you to go into management in this motel chain. We will train you, pay all expenses, and of course there will be a large adjustment in your wages." I then told him that I appreciated the vote of confidence, but I came in that night prepared to give a two-weeks notice because I had found a job in town where I could work during the day. I told him I could spend more time with my family. I thanked him for considering me for the position and said I must leave in two weeks. I expressed to him I didn't think the motel-restaurant business was for me.

When the two weeks passed, which seemed liked two months, I left the motel that morning and did exactly what God told Lot and his family when they left Sodom, I didn't look back. I kept going never to return. I started the job at the drugstore the following Monday. I found myself to be much happier. I was much more at ease with the public, because now I was dealing with hometown folks and they were much kinder.

Chapter 5
The Vision

I began work at the Cartersville Dunaway Drug Store in late February 1978. I was hired into the position of merchandising manager. I had never worked in merchandising before, but they were willing to train me. I spent a great deal of time ordering, unloading, pricing, and shelving the merchandise as it came into the store. There was a room set apart from the main store that was used for storing and pricing the merchandise. I was the only one responsible for this particular job, so I spent a great deal of my time in the storage area, and as a result, was alone most of the time. As I separated and priced the merchandise, I would talk to God. I had many questions concerning His purpose and will for my life. This was always foremost on my mind. I along with Jane continuously sought God for answers and the manifestation of His perfect will.

I enjoyed my work and looked forward to it, but not as intently as when I worked at the carpet mill. It seemed my experiences with the unemployment situation and God's provision had altered my priorities in the real and spiritual world. My working schedule was to open the store at 8 a.m. and work until 2 p.m. The next day I would report at 1 p.m. and work until 9 p.m. This was the schedule each day for two weeks including the weekend. I would get every other weekend off. It wasn't bad because the work wasn't difficult, the employees were fun to work with, and there was always someone in the store. I wasn't completely alone like I was at the motel.

After several months, I was offered a manager's position at one of the Marietta drugstores owned by Mr. Dunaway. It was a significant increase in pay and would have solved a number of our financial problems quickly. I discussed it with Jane, knowing all the time it wasn't God's will. How could I do His will in Cartersville if I lived in Marietta? Somehow I knew His will for me was to be accomplished in Cartersville, not Marietta. Moving was out of the question. On Monday, I called Mr. Dunaway and told him I simply couldn't accept his offer. I had established roots in Cartersville and wasn't willing to move at this time. I told him about the calling I felt God had on my life, and it required me being here, not 25 miles down the road. He very politely said he understood and that was the end of the matter.

Not long after this, the manager of the store where I worked in Cartersville resigned to open his own pharmacy. I was offered the manager's job with the same pay and bonuses I would have received in the Marietta store. I accepted the job, all the time seeing the Divine Hand of God directing our lives. It was now obvious, the previous job offer in Marietta was an attempt by the adversary, not man, to remove me from the picture of God's will being fulfilled. The strongest weapon available was used, money.

In the meantime, Jane had gone to work as church secretary at the Cartersville Church of God. The pastor was out of the office part of the time visiting homes and hospitals and he needed a secretary. As people adjusted to the church having a secretary, they began calling Jane with their prayer needs. In a short period of time she began counseling with individuals, sharing the Word of God into their situation, and praying with them. Some of the load was taken off the pastor. Jane would visit the hospital and counsel with his sheep, allowing him more time to pray and seek God for his messages and wisdom to handle the church.

One day I stopped by the church to see Jane. The pastor was there and asked if we had ever been to Cleveland, Tennessee to visit the Church of God Headquarters. We told him that we had not. He said he was going the next day and asked if we would like to go. We naturally accepted the invitation since it was one of my few days off. The next morning the three of us headed to Cleveland. I was in the front with the pastor and Jane was in the back seat. Desiring desperately to know God's will in my life, I had a fear that I might miss the final call when it came. I asked the pastor, "How did you know when you were called to preach?" He began to explain that while in Lee College a revival was being held. He was concerned about his calling and what God expected of him. On a Sunday evening at the conclusion of the revival he went to the altar asking God for some answers. He said, "While in prayer asking God for answers He spoke this word to me: 'PREACH." That word instantly pierced me like a knife. That was exactly what I had heard in the pulpit that Easter Sunday night while the family and I were singing and narrating *The Three Nails*.

I was petrified. I told the pastor what had happened to me on Easter Sunday night in church, and he said, "I'm not surprised." I was certainly surprised because that was the last thing I wanted to hear. Though I had no preconceived idea what God wanted from me, I certainly didn't want this. I was not a people person, I was not the pastor type, and I just could not see me in that role at anytime for any reason. There was almost rebellion in my

66

attitude. I did not want to preach or have anything to do with it. I fretted and worried about the situation until finally I stored that word "preach" in my subconscious and refused to entertain the idea any further.

It was the continued handiwork of God that provided Jane the job at the church. She was earning $100 a week. This was a tremendous boost to our financial situation since the salary she was making was enough to cover the $75 I had to pay the bank on the interest accumulated while out of work. We finally got the interest current and were able to have a little extra money. I took the children to the drugstore and bought us all a candy bar. To be able to "splurge" without worrying about paying a bill was a true blessing from God. All of us were thankful for the provision God had given, not just the candy, but in every aspect of our lives. We believed God was blessing because of seed we planted even under difficult circumstances. We tithed on every cent that came into our hands as gifts during the time I was unemployed. We also tithed on our only steady income of $20 a week from babysitting. We tithed on every cent that was given to us by anyone because we believed the Word. We felt compelled to give God the first fruits of everything even if it was just two dollars a week. We believed He received it from us as a sacrificial offering and added to our account of blessings on this earth.

One morning in mid-May 1979, I was home alone. It was my day to work the afternoon shift. The children were in school and Jane was at work. I was preparing my lunch before leaving for the drugstore. I got up from the kitchen table and walked toward the stove. Suddenly I felt a presence before me. It was definitely spiritual. It was so powerful I felt unable to go around it, through it, or over it. The impression was a very large object. I had absolutely no idea what it was. I didn't see or hear anything. I just sensed a presence. It lasted about two seconds and was gone. I was not afraid but was certainly mystified. I finished my lunch and went to work. When I arrived I walked to the pharmacy in the back of the store to sign in and let the manager know I was there. As I walked down the aisle there was that "thing" again. It happened exactly the same way as in my kitchen giving me the same sensation. Several times during the day it happened. "Lord, what are you trying to tell or show me?" became my prayer. It didn't matter whether I was at home, at work, or walking down the street. It became more and more real to me in the few days that followed.

After about a week I began to realize the object was a tower. I had absolutely no idea what kind of tower since I knew nothing about them. I knew it was large. It was as if I was standing at the base looking upward to the top, although at this time I had still not seen anything. All of this was feelings and sensations, which can be misleading. I continued seeking God about the matter, wanting to know more and more desperately what was happening and why. I shared with Jane what was taking place but was unable to describe the tower or draw it, since I hadn't seen it. The sensation continued to happen a couple or three times daily. I told no one other than Jane because I felt very uneasy and foolish trying to tell someone I was sensing a tower but couldn't see it, didn't know where it was, or why this was happening. Truthfully, I was fearful about what people would think, so we just kept it to ourselves.

One afternoon while home alone again, the same scenario happened. I was suddenly standing at the base of a "spiritual" tower. This time I looked up and when I did I actually saw the tower. It had alternating colors of red and white. When I saw this in the spirit I knew I was standing at the base of some type of transmitting tower. My immediate thought was, "television transmitter." Once I realized I was in the presence of a transmitting tower, the occurrences ceased and never happened again. I shared with Jane what had happened, but there wasn't any real excitement or elation since neither of us knew anything about a tower or why God had chosen to present this to me. We continued to pray seeking answers but none were forthcoming. There was absolutely no doubt in my mind about what I had seen, but I didn't share it with anyone. We had no answers ourselves and certainly didn't want people guessing. I knew it was a transmitting tower and nobody would be able to convince me otherwise. It had taken root in my spirit and there it was to stay.

On or about May 31, 1979, my pastor asked if I would like to accompany him to a service in the North Georgia Mountains. He had been invited to preach a special service as part of a weeklong revival session the church was conducting. I agreed to go since I was off from work that particular afternoon and evening. During the trip to the church I kept thinking about what had been happening during the last couple of weeks and particularly the last time the tower appeared to me. I was preoccupied and very quiet. He asked if anything was wrong, and I assured him there wasn't.

After the church service was completed he decided to stop in Calhoun, Georgia to get something to eat. We had not eaten before the service and he stated he was very hungry. We stopped at Shoney's. The restaurant was fairly crowded, but the waitress seated us in one of the tables that seats only two. We were the first table on the right upon entering the dining area. Just as we were seated a large number of young people came in. They were all in uniform as if they had come from a basketball game. Since the restaurant was nearly full they had to wait a while before being seated. All of them were mingling and talking directly behind our table.

After giving the waitress our order, I began to share about the happenings of the past two weeks. When I finished he sat there for a moment. He looked at me and said, "Have you been talking to Daniel Holton?" I replied, "No sir." He began sharing with me that Daniel had a burden to build a FM radio station in Cartersville under the auspices of the church for the purpose of broadcasting the gospel. Daniel said he already had the transmitter and was really waiting for God to move. When the pastor spoke those words the Spirit of God fell upon me with a power that I had never felt before. It was as if the heavens had literally opened and the Glory of God, feeling like warm oil, was being poured over me in waves. The voice of God said, "THAT IS WHAT I WANT YOU TO DO. BUILD ME A CHRISTIAN FM RADIO STATION."

I knew at that precise moment what my calling was. I would have a major role in building a Christian radio station in Cartersville, Georgia, to uplift Jesus Christ. I began visibly shaking. The table was literally moving because of my legs jumping up and down. My pastor seated across from me immediately saw what was happening. He kept repeating over and over, "Glory…Glory…Glory." I didn't know, nor did I really

70

care, at that moment whether or not the young people behind me knew or saw what was happening. I really wanted to shout and run, but the better part of wisdom and restraint said to keep my seat. After I settled down and shared with the pastor the words God had spoken, he instructed me to get in touch with Brother Holton and share it with him.

The next day I shared with Jane the happenings of the previous night and the words God spoke to me concerning a FM radio station. She didn't seem to get excited. It was as if she didn't totally hear or receive what I had said. She was standing at the kitchen sink washing the few dishes we had used for breakfast. Suddenly God spoke to her, "THE TOWER WILL BRING LIFE AND LIFT THE SPIRIT. WORDS SPOKEN WOULD CUT DEEPER THAN A TWO-EDGED SWORD. IT WOULD BRING PEACE." She then had a vision of what appeared to her as the top portion of a tower or a tall structure. At the top was an arched dish much like a satellite dish. In the middle portion of the structure was the front of a large boat. God spoke again, "JUST AS THE ARK SAVED PEOPLE FROM THE FLOOD OF DESTRUCTION, SO WILL THE TOWER SAVE MEN FROM THE DEPTHS OF HELL. THIS IS NOT SOMETHING TO BE MOUTHED. IT WILL COME TO PASS. IT WILL EDIFY AND BUILD UP. IT WILL BE A JEWEL IN YOUR CROWN. IT WILL BE SECURE."

God was speaking to Jane about the radio station and at that time planted the vision within her spirit to believe it could and would be accomplished. I had a very real and very deep sense the doors to the remainder of our lives were about to open. We had finally received the purpose for which we were born and put together as husband and wife. This revealing from God was the means of fulfilling His command to me several years earlier to, "SPREAD THE GOSPEL AROUND THE WORLD," "PREACH THE HOLY GHOST," and "PREACH." I had never been more positive of anything in my life. I knew somehow, someway through and by the grace and mercy of the Almighty God, this radio station would come to pass. He had placed within me the faith to believe and pursue His Rhema Word and His command to build a Christian FM radio station in Cartersville, Georgia.

The following Sunday evening the pastor called me to his office before service and asked if I wanted to share with the church what God had spoken. I nervously got up in front of the congregation that evening and shared about the vision God had given Jane and me. I felt somewhat apprehensive announcing it for the first time. Would they believe me? Would they think I conjured all of this up in my own mind? Just what would they think? As I finished sharing they actually applauded. I was in total disbelief. They received what I said and seemingly were very supportive.

On June 4, I visited with Brother Holton at his place of business and shared with him what had happened at Shoney's. He was elated that God had placed the burden of building the station on someone else and was no longer in this by himself. Since I knew nothing about radio, electronics, or the procedure necessary to begin a station, he advised me to learn something about radio and television in order to get a license to operate. He stated that I needed to confer with someone that knew about these things. He recommended an instructor at Coosa Valley Tech in Rome, Georgia. Mr. Holton also stated that he would finance the station, and once it was established the station could pay him back what he had invested in it.

Mr. Ray, the instructor at Coosa Valley Tech, enlightened me tremendously concerning the steps necessary to eventually get an operating license from the Federal Communications Commission. I was concerned about my lack of knowledge in the field of radio and electronics. Mr. Ray stated that a vast amount of electronic knowledge was not necessary. To acquire that knowledge would require two years of schooling. I knew I didn't have two years.

I shared this information with Brother Holton. I began rationalizing in my mind we could put the tower on Ladd's Mountain and the studio at the back of a rather large acreage the church had purchased for a new sanctuary. I was beginning to rationalize we could accomplish a certain thing, do this, do that, put this piece of equipment here and that tower over there. These types of thoughts continued to ravage my mind. I was beginning to try and do all of this organizing and establishing in my own strength and mind, not asking God what He wanted. Daniel and I shared we could build the studio with used equipment and all we really needed was enough power from the station to reach Bartow County. That would keep down cost. We could at a later date update the equipment and the studio as money became available. When I left his place of business, God spoke to me very vividly, "I WANT MY STATION."

As the days passed I began to feel troubled in my spirit. I knew absolutely nothing about radio. My lack of knowledge and feelings of inadequacy became a playground for the devil to torment me. I would hear questions like, "Where are you going to get qualified engineers since you are so ignorant? Where are you really going to build the studio? Do you think the church is going to allow you to use their land? Who is your attorney going to be that knows something about radio? Who will be your financial expert to help raise this up? Where are you really going to put the tower?" My nights became sleepless. Many hours were spent on my prayer stool seeking God for all these answers and more. "Father, do you want me to quit work and become an engineer? How do I do this with so little knowledge? Where do I go, who do I talk to so I can obtain knowledge?" Suddenly through the midst of my troubled thinking and praying God said, "IF YOU BUILD A HOUSE YOU DON'T LEARN TO BE THE CONTRACTOR; YOU HIRE THE CONTRACTOR." Praise God my concern about the lack of electronics knowledge was immediately answered and the anguish lifted. I felt that the Lord was telling me not to concern myself with the details. He would send qualified people, and all I had to do was put it together.

Chapter 6
Putting It Together

On a Thursday night, June 14, 1979, I began to feel the frustrations and doubts concerning my ability creep up on me again. I woke up early Friday morning and asked Jane to pray with me. We asked God to keep our hearts and minds clear and not let satan come in and confuse us. I also asked that He make me sensitive to His Spirit that I may hear His voice and follow His direction. When I finished praying, I heard, "BE PATIENT MY SON. I AM WORKING OUT THE DETAILS." I felt such peace and comfort come over me. I truly felt like a son to the Father. I got up from the stool where I was praying and sat at the kitchen table looking into the morning sun as it rose in the eastern sky. I picked up a pen from the table and began writing what I was sensing and feeling in my spirit.

> *For the first time in my life I feel like a son. God is filling me with His love. The warm rays of sun are like hands of love holding my head and the brightness is as the light of Jesus. The birds singing are like angels voices. God spoke, "MY SON, THIS IS A LITTLE BIT OF HEAVEN."*

On June 22, while working at the drugstore I shared the vision with Mona, a family friend and sister in Christ. She reached into her purse and handed me a ten-dollar bill and said, "This is for the station. I want to be the first one to give." Since God had mercifully taught me to receive, I gladly accepted the money and thanked her many times over. When I got off work I went to the bank and opened a savings account in the name of the station, Immanuel Broadcasting. I decided to put nine dollars in the bank and frame the remaining one dollar as a keepsake for the station that, at this time, only existed by faith. I found a cheap, black frame and framed the dollar as a memento of the first contribution ever made to Immanuel Broadcasting. That framed dollar remains in my office today as a constant reminder of where the ministry was in the beginning, how God has brought it to where it is today and His constant provision that fulfills His Word to the fullest.

The next couple of months were very trying, frustrating, and produced a great deal of anxiety. The Lord spoke to me that the station was not to be put on church property. This negated the need for Ladds Mountain and put a halt to what I thought was instruction from God. I later realized it was my zeal pushing me in an effort to get things done without enough knowledge about the situation. A house was later offered for the studio. After a few weeks it was suddenly no longer available. I began to sense that Daniel and I were at odds concerning the station and its mission. He began to be very apprehensive even to the point of doubting the station would ever come to pass. I began to wonder if my zeal to get things done was creating problems, but things seemed to be moving so slowly. Daniel's knowledge was far superior to mine. He knew what needed to be done, I didn't. I felt a definite barrier between us.

This attitude concerned me since Daniel was the primary source of finances, or at least I thought this at the time. He seemed to be dragging his feet in getting anything completed or making decisions. My zeal was attempting to get something done and things were moving very, very slow. I began thinking maybe God was trying to tell me not to lean on Daniel for finances and knowledge. I should trust Him and only Him. I prayed that God would intervene and melt away any barriers or hard feelings which may have existed and bind us together in love for the calling. I asked that He put us in one mind and accord letting us be in unity. I later spoke with Daniel about what I was feeling and he assured me nothing was wrong, there were no barriers, but he had been preoccupied with another project that was now completed. He would now be able to concentrate his efforts once again on the station. I heard what he said, but for some reason the words did not settle in my spirit because the feelings did not leave.

Several weeks later Daniel and I had an appointment with an attorney to begin the paperwork for a 501(c)(3) tax exemption status from the IRS. When the meeting was over, I left with what I call a broken heart because of comments made during the meeting and the general attitude of Daniel and the lawyer. I felt completely rejected and totally humiliated. The hurt was so deep that expressing it verbally or on paper was almost impossible. The feelings reached down to the bottom of my "gut" and seemed to gnaw and eat. I wanted to go off alone and have a good cry. Thoughts of quitting and letting Daniel and the attorney build and operate the station without my involvement entered my mind. After all I had no money, no knowledge of radio in regard to how to start or operate, no legal knowledge, and I certainly was not a businessman.

During the meeting Daniel and the attorney were making decisions as if I wasn't even in the room. I felt like a thorn in Daniel's flesh or a second thumb. The God-inspired vision was being approached as though it was many years in the future and didn't apply to the present. The general attitude was Daniel's vision was the only vision that was important, and it would take ten years to complete, so the vision God gave me would have to take ten years. Daniel's "vision" was now coming to the forefront. I was hearing things I had never heard before, and I was in shock. Daniel had suggested the number of hours in which operation would take place would only be a few hours each day. My heart was telling me 18 hours a day minimum and eventually 24 hours a day. The attorney said, "That is a vision to be hoped for in the future, something to be worked on later." Their attitude was the station would be a "public-service" station broadcasting local news, sports, moral issues, and contemporary gospel music only. The vision I had was for the station to broadcast sound Bible teaching and play a music mix of southern gospel, inspirational, and contemporary, as well as news. It was to be primarily a music station. I was deeply hurt by the attitude presented. It seemed like a very selfish attitude with the sole purpose of fulfilling an egotistical vision for the sake of professionalism. Where was God in that?

I spent the following week in prayer asking God to somehow touch Daniel and make him see the path He wanted for the station. It was as though Daniel and I were on two separate visions from two separate sources headed in two distinctly different directions. I prayed for God to bring us into one mind and one accord regarding the station and let us get on with the job. One of us was wrong. I prayed, "God if it is me reveal it to me, if it is Daniel please open his eyes." I continued to pray for answers asking God not to let me harbor bitterness and not let anguish build up in my heart. I prayed that Daniel would be made to see beyond his personal wants and desires but look to God for His. The Lord spoke to me, "HE (Daniel) HAS NOT DECREASED." I kept praying, "Lord show us the way. I am aching to fulfill the job you have for me, and I know time is running out."

I had a sense that just as Moses never set foot in the Promised Land but saw it from a distance, so shall I never see the total completion of the vision God has given me, but I felt it would come to pass. I said, "Thank you Father for your patience and may the station be delivered for your Glory."

After several weeks I asked my pastor if I could talk to him. I explained to him my feelings and frustrations about the station and the pace in which it was moving forward. I shared about what appeared to be a double vision and the problems I was having communicating with Daniel and about how inadequate and unqualified I felt to attempt such a task. Not only was my problem with Daniel but also a number of other people, namely Christians. Many expressed their doubts to me about the success of such a venture. Doubts and fears were ravaging my soul as the darts of disbelief kept coming at me. I tried to completely open up and tell the pastor everything.

When I finished he sat there a moment very quietly looking down at his desk. In a moment he raised his head slowly and said, "Brother Ed, did God give you a vision for a radio station or did He not?" I said, "Yes He did." "Are you sure?" he said. "Yes, absolutely," I replied. "Then I suggest you forget about Daniel, stop listening to and trying to please people, and do what God has instructed you to do. You feel inadequate but you must realize that if God calls you to do something, He will equip you to do it. He has called you, so He has already equipped you. You need to trust in Him and the resources He has and will provide through you and to you. It doesn't matter what people think or say, it only matters what God says. Do you believe it can be done?" I said, "I know it can be done. I believe God has placed within me a special faith to believe it will come to pass no matter what comes or doesn't come." We prayed, and I left his office with a renewed confidence, spirit, and faith to know all things were possible with God including the radio station.

In the meantime, I discovered that a consulting engineer would be required to prepare a frequency search to find out if any FM frequencies were available on which to broadcast. After a number of phone calls to existing stations, talking to and visiting a number of people locally finding no help, and after several months had passed, I was finally referred to Mr. James Price of Sterling Communications in Chattanooga, Tennessee. I called Mr. Price and discussed the vision with him. He was extremely courteous, as well as encouraging, and he felt it would be possible. This was very refreshing since all I had been in contact with was discouragement and in some cases obnoxious people. He informed me he knew all of the commercial frequencies were taken but he would do a frequency search on the non-commercial frequencies to check for availability. The fee would be $75 and it would be payable in advance. I agreed, sent him the check, and waited.

A few days passed, and I received in the mail the results of the search. I was somewhat apprehensive to open it but heard in my spirit the words of my pastor,

"Did God give you a vision for the radio station or did He not?" I said to myself, "Of course He did." I ripped the letter open and the contents revealed there were two frequencies available. The first frequency was 91.5 FM. He stated that a station was being applied for in Cumming, Georgia on that frequency so we would be limited in power. The other frequency was 91.7 FM. We could use that frequency and construct a 3,000-watt station. That was the last frequency available between Atlanta and Chattanooga for commercial or non-commercial stations. There could never be another new station constructed in that corridor if we took 91.7 FM. I called Mr. Price and told him, "I'll take it. What is next?" He asked if Jane and I could meet with him at his office in Chattanooga for a discussion on the matter. We made the appointment and anxiously awaited the meeting.

During the meeting Mr. Price explained some "facts of life" to me concerning FM radio and the radio industry in general. It was a real education. He stated we would need a tower location, a studio location, a corporation established with a board of directors, a tax exempt status since we would be non-commercial on that frequency, and of course a corporate name. Since Mr. Price was a Christian and said he liked to work getting Christian stations on the air, I had no problem communicating the vision with him. All of the requirements he needed I did not have except the name. I knew from the beginning that it would be called the Immanuel Broadcasting Network. He said since the lower portion of the FM dial (91.9 down) had been set aside for educational broadcasting and 91.7 was a non-commercial frequency, he felt the FCC would have less questions if we would call it Immanuel Educational Broadcasting Network. Even though

I knew that wasn't what God wanted, I reluctantly agreed to the change. He wanted to know why I spelled Immanuel with an 'I' and not an 'E'. I told him the Old Testament spelling was what I was using. He also stated it would cost $3,000 to prepare and file the application, to be paid in full before filing.

We talked about the power output of the station. He asked if we had money to build a 3,000-watt station. From his information the equipment to be purchased and the operation of a station with a 3,000-watt rating would be very expensive. He commented it would be easier on us financially if we applied for a 100-watt station and increased the power at a later date when money was available. I thought a few minutes and told him okay. He, of course, didn't know at the time, and I sure wasn't knowledgeable enough to see this decision would be a wrong decision and would hurt the ministry for the remainder of its days. I asked if he could start the preparation process if I gave him a check for $2,000 since that was all I had at the moment. He said yes and he would work around the other information until I could get it to him. I wrote him the check leaving just a few dollars in the station account.

Jane and I returned home and began work immediately on the items Mr. Price needed. I secured an attorney and an accountant to begin the legal process with the state and the IRS. Neither of them charged for their services except what they were charged by the state for filing. The forms were quickly filed for the tax exemption status and the corporate status. In the meantime I began searching for a studio location and a broadcast tower. Mr. Price had given me some parameters within which I had to operate. The tower needed to be as high in elevation as possible because the higher the tower the better the FM signal coverage due to the hilly terrain. The studio had to be within eight miles of the tower because of FCC rules regarding signal strength of the city of license, which was Cartersville.

Fred Harris referred me to George Shropshire, the owner of a local company, Bartow Paving. He said that George had a tower on Ponders Mountain for the purpose of communicating with his many trucks and workers he had all over the county. I made an appointment to meet and talk with Mr. Shropshire concerning the use of his tower. He was very favorable and said he would let me use it without cost, but I would have to confer with and get the landowner's permission. I met with the landowner and he was also favorable and said I could use it without cost. Praise God the tower location was secured. I phoned Mr. Price and gave him the information.

Next was the studio. I knew several people who had office space downtown so I conferred with them. One individual had a couple of rooms he said I could use. Since I knew nothing about how much room I needed, I agreed and again it was without cost in the beginning. I called Mr. Price and gave him the address of the proposed studio and told him the legal papers were filed and we were waiting for them to be returned.

By August of 1980 all the paperwork had been received and copies forwarded to the engineer, and as far as I knew Mr. Price was working on the application for Immanuel Educational Broadcasting Network to file with the FCC to build the radio station at 91.7 FM just as God had directed.

A tremendous amount of legwork had to be done obtaining several hundred surveys in person to accompany the application to Washington D.C. for their approval. With the help of several friends we were able to accomplish this in the proper amount of time to send with the application. I had not forgotten I needed an additional $1,000 before he would complete the application. I had determined in my heart I wasn't going to ask for it but God would have to give it like all the other had been given without asking. I waited…and waited…and waited. The holiday season was approaching as 1980 was quickly coming to an end.

On Friday before Thanksgiving, Mr. Price phoned me and said, "I have completed the application but before I can mail it to the FCC, I will need the other thousand dollars. We need to get it in before the end of the year so it will have a 1980 date on it. Maybe the FCC will process it faster since they aren't particularly rushed this time of year. When the New Year comes in, it will then be prior year dated." The bank account had less than $25 dollars in it, and I certainly didn't have the money personally. The following Sunday night in church I labored before the Lord concerning the thousand dollars. I lay on the altar after service crying and pleading with the Lord for His help. I had no way to get the money and the time had come to move forward. I must have lain there for an hour crying hard tears that seemed to come from my innermost being, almost sobbing at times.

Suddenly, I saw the picture of a check. The check was the long business type. I saw the person's name and the amount was $1,000. The name and the amount were written in sterling silver. I got up from the altar with absolute assurance that God was going to supply the

84

money. When I turned around to be seated on the front pew there were still a few people in the church sanctuary talking. Jane was talking to Pat Harris toward the rear of the church and called for me. When I approached them Pat said to me, "Ed, I was supposed to give you this two weeks ago for the station and just didn't do it. Please forgive me." She handed me a check folded in half. Jane and I had grown accustomed to people handing us money for the station. We would not look at it, just put it in our pocket and thank the giver for helping. As Pat handed me the check I naturally put it in my shirt pocket. As I did she said, "No, look at it. It's all right." I removed the check from my pocket and opened it. There was a check for $1,000. It was the same business type check with the same signature I saw in the vision at the altar just a few minutes earlier. I literally broke. This was the largest check the station had received at this point and the most needed at the time. I could hardly stand still for the joy of the Lord was filling my soul, and I realized even more that God had His hand on this station.

The next morning I went to work at the drugstore. I arrived a few minutes early so I could call Mr. Price and tell him I had the money. I reached in my billfold to get his business card so I would have his phone number available. When I saw his card, I was astounded. The name of his company was Sterling Communications. The letters I had seen on the check in the vision the previous evening at church were printed in raised, sterling silver lettering. His business card was printed exactly the same. "My God, how great You are," I said. I could hardly believe my eyes. I was alone in the store at the time and I absolutely shouted, "Praise your Holy Name." When I settled down I called Mr. Price, told him what happened and I was putting his final $1,000 in the mail today. He said, "Good, I will mail your application today and we will see what happens." He said it would take about seven months to process.

Chapter 7
Just In Time

Once the application was filed and accepted by the Federal Communications Commission, all I could do was wait. It was very easy to figure the construction permit should be received sometime in late July or August. I made several attempts to get equipment prices, find an engineer, and get some feel for what I was up against from this point forward. By this time Daniel was no longer involved. I was basically alone. There wasn't anyone in Cartersville with knowledge about the needs and requirements of FM radio. I didn't know who to go to. I called a few equipment companies that I read about in a broadcasting magazine, but they wouldn't talk to me until I received the construction permit to build the station. I finally realized I had to wait for everything until the permit was issued.

Finally on August 19, 1981, the Federal Communications Commission approved the construction permit for Immanuel Educational Broadcasting to build a FM station in Cartersville. When I received my copy of the permit a few days later, it stated the station must be on the air by August 19, 1982, one year later. My next step was to determine the call letters for the station. The Federal Communications Commission requested five sets of call letters in preference order. They would assign the first available set for use. My first request was WBFJ - We're Broadcasting For Jesus. My second was WCCV - We're Cartersville's Christian Voice. When the FCC returned the choices to me a few weeks later they had assigned WCCV.

Now another wait began with a number of questions. Where would I put the studio? How much money would I need to build WCCV? Where would I find a good engineer? Who would be the announcers? All types of questions began to arise. I decided since God had gotten us to this point, He would handle the remainder. As people heard and began to realize we now had governmental approval to construct the station, they began giving money more freely. I was accumulating several thousand dollars in the bank but still didn't know how much I needed. Days turned to weeks, weeks turned to months. As August 19 approached I began to get concerned. During the spring of 1982, I made a determined effort to locate an engineer. In May I was given the name Steve Schrader as a possibility. He was the engineer for one of the local AM stations. I contacted him and explained my circumstances to him. We made an appointment to meet one evening at a local restaurant to discuss the matter.

During the meeting I was in for another education concerning radio. He began explaining what kind and how much equipment would be needed. I then asked the all-important question, "How much money do I need?" He thought a minute then replied, "About $47,000 for all new equipment and going stereo. If you want to use refurbished equipment and broadcast in mono I can probably get it for $10,000 less. I do not suggest you go mono because stereo is the thing in FM broadcasting and mono will make you look and sound antiquated. I can get used equipment, but there are no guarantees, and some of the lesser equipment will compromise the quality FM sound." I was stunned. It was as if someone had used a stun gun on me. I was speechless. In a few moments when I was able to speak I said, "Steve, I don't have anything near that kind of money. I don't know what to do." "Why don't you think about it for a few days? We still have some time left. Call me and let me know," was his reply.

The station and the resources needed to get it on the air were all I could think about for a few days. Several days later Steve called me at work and said, "I have some good news and some bad news. I can get all the equipment you need in stereo and brand new for $37,000." That was a relief and certainly some good news. He went on to say, "Because you are not established in the industry they will have to have cash in hand before they will deliver." That obviously was the bad news. I told him okay, I would call him, and thanked him for his time and trouble. At this point in time he may as well been quoting a $370,000 figure. I only had a few thousand in the bank, and I knew we would need operating capital once we signed on the air. I said to myself, "Well God, here we are. You are going to have to move in this situation. You know I don't have that kind of money." All I could do was wait and worry. Yes, worry, a perfectly natural human response to desperation, and I was certainly feeling desperate.

Time was running out. In addition to ordering the equipment and having it delivered there was also installation time to get the station ready. Steve had a job in Atlanta and could work at WCCV only in the evening. I became conscious of the deadlines placed by the Federal Communications Commission. Looking at the calendar I could see time was almost gone. I called Steve and asked if we could get an extension to the expected completion date. He said, "If you have the equipment ordered but the station is not ready to sign on, the Federal Communications Commission will usually give a six month extension. That is usually their limit unless you have some unusual circumstances. Having no money is not one of those circumstances."

Meanwhile a gentleman called me one afternoon and asked if I was the individual wanting to build a radio station in town. I told him I was. He said he thought he may have a place and wanted to know if I could come and look at it. It was located in the Cowan Building in downtown Cartersville. I looked it over and knew it would be perfect with some modifications. I reluctantly asked what he was asking for the rent, and he said, "$200 a month." This was a great deal less than the figure I was expecting due to the location downtown. I agreed. I inquired how he knew about me looking for a place. He said someone told him about the station, and he immediately thought about the space we had just seen. Now a major hurdle was out of the way. There was now a studio from which to operate.

The month of July had begun. I had about $4,000 for operations. I was crying out to God, "What do I do? Where do I go? I need $37,000 and haven't a clue. Will it even come? Is this the end of the road? Were you just checking my obedience? God, please, help me." I was at an absolute loss. I was at the end of my rope.

July was now gone and August 19 was rapidly approaching. I was almost in a panic. I decided to go to the bank and talk to the bank president. I knew him, and we had talked on several occasions about personal matters. This was the first time I approached him regarding the station. As I walked into the bank I could feel a different attitude in the air. It was as if everyone was much more busy than usual. People were conferring with each other. It was somewhat like a panic feeling. It was not good. People seemed very preoccupied, more than usual, as if something was going on that wasn't particularly good. Not being a banker, I didn't concern myself with what seemed to be going on. I asked to see the president. He was busy at the time, and the secretary asked me to be seated. He would be with me in a moment. I did as instructed. My intention was to ask for a $37,000 loan so the station could be installed. While waiting for my turn to see the president, I was praying for God to open this door so I could get on with what He had called me to do. Just as the president walked to where I was sitting, God spoke to me, "DON'T GO ON THE AIR IN DEBT." The president of the bank asked what I needed and I told him, but I also told him that I no longer had the need. He said, "Ed, I wouldn't advise anyone to borrow money at this time because the interest rate just hit 21%." I said, "Twenty-one percent, no wonder God didn't want me to borrow any money." I told him what had happened and left the bank.

My time was now measured in weeks before the construction permit would expire. I had a relatively small amount in the checkbook, certainly not enough to purchase equipment. All I could do was pray and seek God for answers. I said to myself, if He said don't go on the air in debt, He must have a solution to the problem. However, God was not allowing me to be in on that equation.

One early August morning I was at home alone praying desperately for an answer. Suddenly, I heard a man's name. I knew of the individual but had never met him. I knew he was wealthy and a very strict businessman.

I truly didn't know what to do about what I heard so I left it alone. I got up from where I was praying and went to the church where Jane was working. As I walked into her office, the pastor walked out of his and asked if there was anything he could do. I asked him to pray for the situation and me because I had about two weeks remaining and all would be lost. He said, "Brother Ed, come into my office and let's pray now." I agreed and we went into his office. He had two wingback chairs in front of his desk. We knelt down in front of those chairs and started to pray. We weren't praying 30 seconds and he said, "God just gave me a name." I said "Who?" He said, "John Hodge." Very exited I said, "That's the same name He gave me 20 minutes ago. Do you know him?" He replied, "Certainly, we have talked and had lunch on several occasions." He said to Jane, "Sister Tuten, call Mr. Hodge's secretary, Mary Eliza, and make an appointment for Brother Ed and me to meet with him." The appointment was set for the next morning at Mr. Hodge's office.

We met with Mr. Hodge the next day. I noticed the date because of time being so short. I was counting days now because the deadline was near and I still had no answers. I had exactly two weeks remaining to the day and the construction permit would be cancelled. When we arrived I found Mary Eliza and Mr. Hodge to be very cordial people making me feel very comfortable. Usually I was very intimidated by people that had money. The pastor introduced me and asked me to share with Mr. Hodge what God had spoken to me to do. I didn't really know how he would respond, but I told him everything I could remember. When I finished Mr. Hodge said to me, "Son, I want you to see how much money you can raise in a week then come back next Thursday." I, of course, said I would. Upon leaving his office I thanked the pastor for his assistance and left for work. During my drive to the drugstore I thought to myself, "By next Thursday there will be only four days remaining." I knew I wasn't going to ask anyone for money during this week so anything raised would be as in the past. People would have to just give it.

Thursday finally came and I was a nervous wreck. The pastor was unable to accompany me to see Mr. Hodge, so this was a trip I had to take alone. Jane was busy at the church and was unable to accompany me. When I arrived at his office I was greeted as if I had known them all my life and were life-long friends. This helped settle me down and we talked for a few moments. Mr. Hodge finally asked, "Well, how much were you able to raise this week." I told him, "$600." He said, "That's more than I thought you would raise." He hesitated for a moment, turned to me and said, "How much do you need to put the station on the air?" I said, "$37,000." He looked at Mary Eliza, his secretary and bookkeeper, and said, "Give him what he needs." I was floored. I said, "Sir, I can't pay you back that kind of money. I don't have it, and it will take a long time for the station to get in a financial position to pay you back." He said, "Son, this is not a loan. It is a gift. Now get on with what God has called you to do." Tears overwhelmed me. I couldn't believe my ears. "My God what have You done?" Through the tears I kept thanking Mr. Hodge over and over and over. Seeing my emotional condition and apparently trying to help me along he said, "Go on now and get to work." Mary Eliza wrote the check and handed it to me. As I was leaving his office I kept thanking him until the door was closed behind me. When I got to my car, I really let go. My emotions and my spirit were at a pinnacle of praise, and I couldn't offer enough thanks to God. I couldn't praise Him enough for the miracle He had just performed. I went to the church and told Jane. We rejoiced and praised God more, thanking him for His grace and mercy. Thanking Him for fulfilling His Word and supplying the need.

I finally got to work at the drugstore and immediately called Steve, the engineer. I told him we had the money and to order the equipment then file with the FCC a request for an extension of time. We now qualified for it since the equipment was ordered. He said, "Where did you get that much money that quick? Did you borrow it?" I told him what had happened, and he was in total disbelief. It was a true witness to him that this ministry was in God's hands and not his, mine, or anyone else's. It was August 15, two days before my birthday and four days before scheduled cancellation of the construction permit to build WCCV. By the time the equipment was ordered and the request for an extension of time was prepared and delivered to the FCC, it was August 18. One day before cancellation. I said to myself, "That was a close call." I witnessed first hand God was not early nor was He late, but just in time. I was beginning to learn this attribute of the Almighty. I thought to myself, "Lord, since all of this has happened this way and we are this close to the end of the year, I would like to sign on Christmas Day with the words "Happy Birthday Jesus" and present to You the Christian station that was called out of the dust of the earth." That desire, however, was never to be. It wasn't in God's plan.

Chapter 8
The Miracle

In the meantime God continued to provide for my family. The house payment was finally current and our basic financial situation was beginning to stabilize. In May 1981, while trying to get all the information together for the application to be filed with the FCC, I went to work for the Cartersville Post Office as a clerk. I had taken and passed the postal exam two years earlier and simply waited for an opening to become available. During my tenure at the drugstore, one of the employees had mentioned that the exam was being given. I knew being employed by the U.S. Postal Service would be more stability, better pay, and better working hours, not to mention better retirement. The other employee and I decided we would give the exam a try. After all, what did we have to lose? We went to the post office and registered. A few days later we received the date and location of the exam. It was to be held in Atlanta several weeks from the date we received the notice.

One morning when I reported to work at the drugstore, I went to the stock room where I would be alone and I prayed, "God, I want that job with the post office." He replied, "DO YOU WANT IT BAD ENOUGH TO FAST FOR IT?" I said, "Yes." He said, "FAST SEVEN DAYS." I thought, "That's tough. I have never fasted more than a few days, but here goes." I began the fast the next day drinking nothing but water. The headaches, the nausea, the not feeling good almost overwhelmed me, but it was as if I didn't have a choice, especially since God had spoken the way He did. Those choices were don't eat and you will get the job, eat and you won't. I feared God too much to try. I went day to day without complaining, really wanting to eat, but I didn't.

When the seven days were over I had pretty much lost my appetite and didn't really care whether I ate or not. I did however eat pizza, my favorite, and didn't get sick. That alone was a miracle. I went to work the next day and reported to the stock room for prayer as I had many times in the few years I had been at the drugstore. I said, "God, I did what you said. The seven days are over." He said, "YES, AND THE JOB IS YOURS." I didn't know at the moment I was about to endure another of those waiting tests. I thought as soon as the fasting was complete, His Word about the job being mine would take effect immediately. Boy, was I wrong. Time passed and finally the employee with whom I'd taken the exam and I received word that both of us had passed the exam and we would be placed on the roster. We thought it would just be a few weeks and we would be out of the drugstore and into the post office. That didn't happen. Weeks, months, and finally a year passed and neither of us had received a word. I began to wonder, "Did I really hear God's voice or was I just wishing." I tried to immediately discount that thought, because I knew what I had heard. As time marched on, it became increasingly difficult to hang on to God's word, but I knew I had no choice regardless of the thought processes that came or what people said at the post office about no jobs being available. "I have a job at the Post Office. It has not materialized, but I know it is mine." Those were the thoughts I kept hanging onto and the words I kept speaking, because I knew God had spoken.

Finally around the first of May 1981, I received a notice in the mail from the postmaster to report to the

Cartersville Post Office for an interview. I was one happy young man. I reported on the requested date and was interviewed by the postmaster and the supervisor. It was a very cordial and relaxing interview with the questions mainly directed at my background and qualifications. Before I left I was asked if I thought I could work for them. I replied, "I don't look at it as working for anyone but working with them to get a job done." The postmaster said we have a few more to interview and we will call you tomorrow. I knew by the spirit when I left his office, the job was mine. God had spoken and I believed, but now I could feel it.

The next afternoon the postmaster called me at home and said, "Ed, when can you start work? The job is yours." I told him I had to give a two-weeks notice at the drugstore, and then I could come. I returned to the drugstore and called the owner in Marietta and asked if I could talk to him. He was already on his way to the store for his weekly trip. When he arrived, I shared with him about the post office job and I was giving a two-weeks notice. He said, "Ed, what are they paying you? Is there anything I can do to change your mind?" I said, "My starting salary is $6,500 a year more than I am making here with bonuses plus the insurance and retirement benefits." He said, "I can't compete with the post office. I wish you all the luck in the world. We enjoyed having you as our employee." Upon turning in my notice, the worst part of the resignation process was over. The two weeks passed quickly. On May 16, 1981, I began fifteen years of employment at the Cartersville Post Office just as God had promised two years earlier.

With the construction permit in hand, money given for the equipment, a studio available, an engineer on hand, and a good paying job, I just knew we were on the way to complete victory. The engineer, Steve, had filed with the FCC for the extension and within a month we received the approval adding six months to the construction permit time limit. This gave us until March 1983 to have WCCV on the air. It also gave some breathing room to get things completed in an organized manner. I hired a carpenter to make the few changes needed in the studio. Steve would come in the evening when he got off work in Atlanta to work on the station getting equipment installed and building cabinets. It was a mammoth undertaking, and I was absolutely no help in getting things accomplished because all of this was well over my head. I would spend time with him in the evening while he worked asking a lot of questions. During this time he taught me more about FM radio than I would have learned in any school.

As Steve neared completion I could see there was a remote chance we could sign on Christmas Eve or Christmas Day, as I had wanted to do a few years earlier. Steve agreed it was possible if all of the equipment arrived on time. He had the studio completely built. Now he had to wire in all the equipment at the transmitter house we had built on Ponders Mountain to house the multi-thousand dollars worth of equipment needed at that site for broadcasting. One day he called me at work and told me the antenna had not arrived and in a few days all would be complete but that installation. He said he had checked with the manufacturer, and it had been shipped in time to have already been here. The truck line was unable to locate it at any terminal in the country. This was a $9,000 piece of equipment, and it couldn't be located. It was impossible to broadcast without it.

While waiting for the antenna to be found, I hired an announcer, Wayne Frye, to operate the station and basically get everything prepared to sign on. I certainly didn't know what to do, and he had worked at one of the AM stations in Cartersville for a number of years. He was a new Christian and was excited about being a part of WCCV and Christian broadcasting. He began contacting record companies and programming agencies to send music and programs to audition and air. We began developing a small music library with 45 rpm and LP records for airplay.

Thanksgiving, Christmas, and New Year's came and went, still no antenna. The truck lines had exhausted all their resources in trying to locate it. They had the manifest showing it was loaded in South Dakota where it was built but lost track of it after that. The truck lines and Steve were ready to file an insurance claim and have another antenna built. The six-month deadline set by the extension granted by the FCC was about ten weeks away, and Steve was concerned for two reasons. Could another antenna be built, shipped, and installed in time for the deadline? Secondly, if the deadline were missed would the FCC grant another extension? He had never experienced this and was not sure of the possible outcome. The situation was getting serious, and this was the only obstacle keeping us from signing the station on the air.

All of our friends, church members, and anybody that could pray including the prayer and counseling center at the Christian Broadcasting Network (CBN) were fervently praying for answers to the problem. On Tuesday, January 18, I received a call at the post office. The voice on the other end said, "Are you WCCV?" I said,

"No, but I am trying to build a radio station by that name, why?" He replied, "I am the dispatcher for the truck line located on Hwy 411 here in Cartersville. We have a rather large container that has been here for almost a month. It didn't have a shipping address and no one ever claimed it. We finally decided to open the container and the bill inside had WCCV and a name on it. Are you Ed Tuten?" I knew immediately that the antenna had been located. I told the dispatcher I was Ed Tuten, and as soon as I got off work I would be there to check it out. I called Steve at work and told him what had happened. He said, "I'll be there in 45 minutes."

When he arrived we went to the truck line, and sure enough there it was, the long-lost antenna. The shipping label had been mistakenly torn off the container after arriving in Cartersville, and they were waiting for someone to claim it. We claimed it, loaded it on the back of Steve's truck, and took it to Ponders Mountain. When we arrived at the tower site and unloaded it, Steve informed me he had already located a tower man to install the antenna and he would be here tomorrow. I was one happy Christian. Finally, sign on was days away. I was excited but also starting to get a little nervous.

On Thursday, January 20, Steve called me at home and said, "Ed, I have the station on the air in the test mode making sure all components are working properly. Why don't you drive around and listen then come here to the tower site and tell me how it sounds?" I yelled, "Jane, it's on the air, listen." I turned our radio to 91.7 FM and there it was. He wasn't playing Christian music but that was okay. This was only a test. Jane and I stood there looking at the radio, hugging each other with tears rolling down our cheeks. We were finally there. We rode around in the car for an hour before he turned it off. We then went to the tower site very excited. Words can't express the exhilaration Jane and I felt as we drove up the mountain road to the transmitter house where Steve was making some last minute adjustments. He said, "How did it sound?" "It was fantastic. It sounded great. The quality and the stereo separation were excellent," I replied. He said, "Good, you are ready to sign on any time you want to." Jane and I looked at each other. I said, "Let's do it Monday, January 24, at 6:00 p.m." Steve said, "Great let's do it." Little did Jane and I know the greatest test of our faith was about to take place in a matter of hours. We returned home and told everyone we knew we were finally signing on the air Monday. I called all the people we knew who had been praying and we shouted it from the housetops. God's Word was finally coming to pass. I made arrangements with the post office to be off on that grand and glorious day and anxiously waited for the day to arrive.

Friday night I didn't sleep very well, being excited as well as nervous. I was up and down seemingly all night long finally getting to sleep about 4 or 5 a.m. I slept until 8:30 or 9:00 Saturday morning. I got up to my usual routine of coffee, getting showered, and dressed. I was going to the station to look at what God had done and to pray, seeking His face for wisdom and understanding for the future. I had no idea what to do next after the station went on the air. As I was putting on my shoes, I turned on the television just in time to hear, "The United States Weather Bureau has issued ice storm warnings for north Georgia for tonight. Rain will begin after dark and with the temperature falling below freezing the rain will freeze as it touches cold surfaces. It will be particularly noticeable on trees, power lines, bridges, and overpasses. As the night progresses some roads may become ice covered. It is suggested that preparations be complete before sunset. Driving after dark is not recommended. The worst area will be from Atlanta north to the Tennessee state line. Stay tuned for further statements."

I was stunned, almost paralyzed, as I stood to my feet in total disbelief. "They don't know what they are talking about," I thought. I yelled for Jane. "Did you hear that?" "No, what is it?" she said. "An ice storm is coming tonight. Do you know what an ice storm will do to a radio station?" I exclaimed as if it was her fault. "I am going to the mountain. I will be back shortly." I got in the car and began the 10 or 12 mile drive to the tower site. All the way there I kept saying over and over, "I can't believe this… I can't believe this." I knew I had better believe it. The weather was cold. The sky was cloudy and the wind was blowing.

As I reached the mountain road going up to where the tower was located, I unlocked the gate and kept going over and over in my mind what elements were necessary to make this station work. Steve had taught me a great deal. In my mind I could see the three telephone lines. One for the right channel, one for the left channel of the stereo signal, and one for a communications line between the studio and the transmitter so it could be remotely controlled. There were power lines coming up the side of the mountain to supply power to all the equipment. There was the expensive equipment, not to mention the concrete blockhouse and the steel door.

As I arrived, I stopped the car and sat there for a moment. There was no one within miles. It was God and me on top of that mountain. There were three towers at that site other than ours. Although the tower didn't belong to us, I would always refer to the tower we were using as ours. One of the towers belonged to the state patrol and was 300 feet tall. The other two were about the size of ours, 190 feet. I got out of the car, closed the door, and stood there for a moment in awe. The wind was blowing very hard. It was difficult to stand without holding on to something. Looking up toward the top of the 300-foot state patrol tower, I could see the tower slightly twisting as the wind was howling through the trees and over the mountain without letting up. The wind would blow past the guy wires that were supporting the tower. The wires would cut the wind like a knife and a loud whistling noise would result sounding like a scream. The howling and roaring accompanied by the high-pitched whistle was deafening. I looked at our tower. It was doing the same thing, slightly twisting as the wind blew past it. The other towers were receiving the same treatment. The sight and sound was powerful. It was awesome and very frightening. I felt very small at the enormity of the power and energy displayed on that mountain that day. I momentarily thought what it must have been like for Moses on the mountain with the presence of the Almighty God Himself.

I began walking to the transmitter house with the wind to my back seemingly pushing me into the house. As I unlocked the door, went in, and closed the door behind me, the powerful sound of the wind was silenced. It was quiet in the little house. Not a sound could be heard. It was as if the wind had stopped, although I knew it hadn't. I dropped to my knees and cried out to God, "Please Lord, we have come too far for

103

all of this to be destroyed in one night. Oh, Lord, help me to understand what is going on. Show me how to pray." After a moment I stood and walked the few steps to the phone box where all the terminals were located for the phones. I laid my hands on the terminal box and prayed for the phone lines to be secure and not be destroyed. I turned to the electric panel, laid my hands on it and prayed for all the electric lines to remain in tact and for power to continue to flow in the morning. I turned to the transmitter, laid my hands on it and prayed for it to be spared the wrath of this storm. I then backed away from the phone box, the electric panel and the transmitter, bowed my head and said, "God, it is up to You. I don't know what else to do."

I opened the door to the screaming, roaring wind and the biting cold. I closed and locked the door then started toward the car. About half way to the car I remembered the tower and the antenna. I had not prayed for them. I turned and walked toward the tower again, the wind to my back seemingly pushing me toward it. As I reached the base of the tower, I grabbed two of the three legs on the tower, clutching them in my hand. I looked up toward the top of the tower. As I did the vision I had in my kitchen a few years ago of a broadcasting tower suddenly became alive. It was real. I was looking at the manifestation of a vision. It had come to pass. Looking up I yelled to the top of my voice to drown out the wind, holding the tower legs like my life depended on it, attempting to shake the structure as if it could hear me, "In the name of Jesus, you will not fall this night." I stood there a moment holding the tower legs with a clinched fist as if I was keeping the 198-foot tower from falling. Finally, I released the tower legs and went to my car.

I went down the mountain, locked the gate, went home, and waited. I was really waiting for the weather bureau to cancel the storm warnings but that didn't happen. Man had given money, man had installed the equipment, man had prayed, but there was absolutely nothing man could do now. It was totally and completely in God's hand to do as He willed. I had done all I could do. If I told you I didn't worry about it all evening, I would be telling something other than the truth. I prayed and worried and prayed most of the evening. I would occasionally check outside after it got dark to see if the rain had begun. The weather bureau was hanging on to its promise, and I was trying my best to hold on to God's. I know what I heard when He said to build it, and I knew it wasn't complete until it went on the air. Nevertheless, I had doubts and I had fears. "Had I done something wrong that God was going to make me back up and do something over? Did I not do something I was supposed to do and missed Him? Had I sinned and He no longer wanted or needed me?" All evening I wrestled with the devil and the thoughts. I wasn't worth anything to anyone including my family.

I thought, "My God, where is the faith of Abraham that he could offer his son on an altar after a promise? Yet this newly born station wasn't going to get a chance to even speak its first word. My Lord, please help me understand." Being a young Christian I took on a defeated attitude and felt all hope was seemingly lost. God was using this situation to teach Jane and I no matter how desperate it seemed, He was still in control. At the time however, I didn't know this. I finally went to bed about

11:00 p.m. I was so exhausted from the day's activities I went right to sleep. I didn't dream. I didn't hear God or anyone else speak to me. I just slept. The next thing I knew the sun woke me early Sunday morning. I jumped out of bed, ran to the door, and looked outside. The sun was shining very bright. There was no ice anywhere. In the trees, on the cars, on the power lines...there was no ice. I called for Jane waking her up about as excited as I could get and said, "Look, Jane, no ice!! They were wrong. We escaped. The ice storm missed us. It didn't happen. Praise God! Praise God! Praise God!" We were two happy people and couldn't wait to get to church and praise God again for what he had done.

I taught Sunday school at that time. The age group was the post-high school, pre-college age. I had about 60 students in my class. It was a joy to teach them because they were eager to learn and usually very prompt and studious. I was always a little early so I could collect my thoughts before they came in while getting my notes in order for the lesson. As they began to come in, Jane and I were of course extremely happy and joyous. Before the class started they began talking and sharing with each other like they usually did. I wasn't really paying much attention. One student talking to another student said, "Did you hear about all those towers that fell on Ponders Mountain last night?" I immediately spoke up and said, "What did you say?" He said, "The radio announced this morning that the towers on Ponders Mountain fell last night." I said, "Why? We didn't have any ice." He replied, "No, there wasn't any here in town but at the higher altitudes there was a lot of ice. The rural area called Center on the other side of Ponders Mountain is without

106

power and many power lines are down on the higher mountains."

It seemed as if the breath of life went out of me. I looked at Jane and said, "After church we will ride up there and see for ourselves." I finished the class even thought my mind and heart was at the mountain. I got through it by God's grace. Church wasn't any better. It seemed like we were in the sanctuary all day. I wanted to go to the mountain and I didn't want to go. My emotions were a wreck. Finally, church was over. Jane, Denise, Howard, and I loaded up the car and the journey began. The children were absolute jewels. They didn't say one word. They knew I was upset. As a matter of fact, it was unusually quiet in the car.

Normally, when driving north on Highway 41, the main thoroughfare in Cartersville, you could see the 300-foot state patrol tower primarily because it had a blinking red light on top. I didn't want to look. I didn't want to know. I kept my line of sight straight ahead in front of the car. As we approached Center Road, the road to the tower sight, I refused to look up but looked only straight ahead and down toward the road as much as possible and remained on the road. As we approached the mountain road I still did not look up. I honestly didn't think I could handle this. I felt as though the end had surely come. When we arrived, the gate it was unlocked as if someone was at the site where the towers were located. Towers were the only thing located on the mountain. I didn't know any other reason for it to be open. On the way to the top Jane began praying in the Spirit. God spoke to her and said, "TODAY YOU HAVE WITNESSED A MIRACLE." She shared it with me, but at the moment I couldn't see a miracle anywhere. All I could see was ice.

As we arrived at the top of the mountain the trees were covered with ice. They were bent over, so heavily laden that some of the tops of the younger pine trees were actually touching the ground. Ice was everywhere. As I pulled up to the site there was twisted steel, guy wires, and broken trees lying on the ground as if a bomb had dropped. The 300-foot state patrol tower had come down and was nothing but a mass of metal on the ground.

I was speechless. I turned and looked at our transmitter house and the door was opened. Out walked Steve. By this time we had gotten out of the car. I walked toward him, and he said the most beautiful words I had heard in a long time. Oddly enough the same words God had spoken to Jane just three minutes earlier. "Ed Tuten, this day you have witnessed a miracle. Not only is our tower the only one left standing. All the equipment, the electricity, and the phone lines are in perfect working order. They were not hurt in any way by the ice. I don't know how this happened, but when the state patrol tower came down it didn't just crumble, it whipped as the top came down first. It took the tops out of the trees around it and brought down the other two towers. We are only about 150 feet from where that tower stood. There is no way that it could have missed our tower." I said, "Steve, you said I had witnessed a miracle. Truly we have. God was with me on this mountain in a powerful way yesterday. I experienced Him. Last night I believe He ordered His angels to watch over His radio station." He said, "I guess so." I asked, "Can we still sign on tomorrow?" He said, "Yes, there is no reason you can't."

From that day until now I have, in my heart, always called Ponders Mountain by its spiritual name. It is

Immanuel Mountain. The reason, God was with us that day and it will forever ring in my heart that maybe, just maybe, I had a mini-Moses experience, not on Mount Sinai in Arabia, but on Immanuel Mountain in Bartow County, Georgia. It was meant for me to never forget no matter how dire the circumstances or how far down I seem to go, God is still in control of His radio station.

On Monday, January 24, 1983, a small group of people gathered in the lobby that had one desk and one chair. The remainder of us stood and shared about the station and how good God was and how faithful He was to His Word. Denise, Howard, Jane, and I stood together in front of the supply room door waiting for the last few minutes before 6:00 p.m. The small, cheap radio was set on 91.7 FM waiting for the first notes of the song, *Jesus, Name Above All Names,* which was to be the sign on signature for WCCV. Wayne Frye, the young man I had hired before Thanksgiving, was in the control room, his hand on the button with everything checked out. It was ready to go.

At 6:00 p.m. the beautiful worship music began filtering over the speakers of that small radio. Jane and I began to weep. There were hugs and tears all over the room that night. As the song continued to play, I had previously recorded the following message to be aired in conjunction with the song.

> *"Good Evening, This is WCCV Cartersville Georgia beginning its broadcasting career. Our studio and offices are located in the Cowan Building on East Main Street in downtown Cartersville with*

transmitting facilities on Ponders Mountain. At 91.7 on your dial WCCV purposes to serve the community and surrounding area uplifting the name of Jesus Christ and bringing you quality Christian Programming until that great and glorious day of His return. I'm Ed Tuten asking you to stay with us now as we join hands with God in prayer and in supplication dedicating this facility to the glory and honor of Almighty God and to His Son, our Savior Jesus Christ.

As the opening song and message ended there was jubilation in the studio. God had brought His will and purpose to completion. We just stood around most of the evening basking in the Glory of the Lord radiating from the radio as praise and worship continued to flow from its speakers. The phones began to ring. People were telling us they could hear it in their cars and in their homes. Different cities immediately around Cartersville such as Emerson, White, and Adairsville were represented in those phone calls. Jane and I were ecstatic. The job was done. Finally God's will was complete. Little did I know this was just the beginning and had absolutely no idea what the future held for the radio station or us.

Chapter 9
The Journey Begins

Our first evening of broadcasting was complete. God received all the Glory humanly possible to offer. The exaltation and praise was unceasing as it filled the airways. Now it was time to begin the day-to-day operation continuing to praise Him for what He had done to get us to this point.

Wayne and I were at the station at 5:45 a.m. the next morning to sign on. Our schedule of operation was 6:00 a.m. until 10:00 a.m. on the air, sign off at 10:00 a.m. until 2:00 p.m., and then resume broadcasting from 2:00 p.m. until 6:00 p.m. Wayne was the only employee, because I was working a full-time job at the post office. As a few short weeks progressed, people began asking us to close in the four hours at the top of the day. Wayne was physically unable to handle an air shift twelve hours a day and do behind the scenes work necessary to keep a radio station on the air. A decision was made to hire another employee to work the afternoon. Vince Hawks was brought on board to assist. He had past radio experience and was a great asset to the ministry on and off the air.

I soon realized the few thousand dollars in the checking account wasn't going to last forever. As payroll, utilities, rent, and other operating expenses began to siphon away the bank balance, my thoughts drifted toward, "What is next? What do I do now?" We were a non-commercial station. That meant the commercial way of doing business as most other radio stations was illegal and our only source of income was going to be from the people. This was called "Public Support." I had no idea what to do. This was as new to me as radio was when God spoke to me a few years ago.

I was not a businessman. I was not a radioman. I was just an individual that heard a voice say, "BUILD ME A CHRISTIAN FM RADIO STATION." Here it is and now what do I do with it? I could feel desperation coming upon me again coupled with a sense of loneliness and wandering without instruction. There were two people on the payroll, Wayne and Vince, depending on WCCV for their livelihood and the money was running out. There was no visible source of income and not a clue as to how to get any. I had already said I would not borrow for operation purposes, and I was not going to beg. I began to develop an attitude that now seems almost rebellious. I was thinking to myself, "This is God's station, let Him take care of it. I can't." My attitude didn't help the situation at all, and things were getting worse with each passing day. Over the air everything seemed fine. Listeners didn't know from my perspective that WCCV had a very short life and was seemingly coming to an end. Ministry continued to go forth. Music, praise and worship, prayer, scripture reading, teaching, and instruction from the Bible were entering into the homes, automobiles, and businesses over the small listening area. All the elements I felt God wanted for this Christian station were being broadcast on a daily basis.

One afternoon, in the midst of this despair, while driving to the station after my shift at the post office was completed, I was thinking about the finances and the desperate condition we were in. Suddenly God spoke to me, "PRAY FOR YOUR OWN FACILITIES." "What did you say?" I asked without hesitation. "Pray for our own facilities?" repeating what I knew I heard. Needless to say

I was irate. "What do you mean pray for our own facilities when I don't have money to pay payroll?" I heard not a word, not a whisper from God. The words the Lord spoke added to the frustration. I knew purchasing our own facility was a virtual impossibility. I was almost angry, but in time I pushed those words to the back of my mind. Always remembering, never forgetting that maybe someday in the future yet unseen, we would have our own facilities and not have to pay rent.

I have since learned God was teaching me His plan of walking by faith. He was showing me little by little how His plans, His economy, and His words would mold and make this ministry into a ministry of His building and His character. This statement about our own facilities was the first instruction of several that eventually involved broadening the coverage area or boarders of WCCV and later Immanuel Broadcasting Network.

Several days after He spoke to me about our facilities, I was working at the post office. I received a phone call from Mary Eliza, the secretary to Mr. John Hodge. She asked if Jane and I could visit Mr. Hodge the next afternoon. We, of course, agreed. He had become a friend to both of us and we had visited his home on several occasions. He was confined at home due to physical reasons so we visited as much as possible without wearing out our welcome or tiring him. Although he gave the money in the beginning to start the ministry, I didn't feel obligated to him in any way. That was the way he wanted it. Jane and I just loved him for who he was and the concern he showed for the ministry and us. He always made us feel very welcome and comfortable, although he was a man of wealth. This didn't seem to bother me. It didn't seem important. He was a man trying to express his love to two people that had nothing and lived payday to payday.

When we arrived at his home on that mid-December evening we were as usual received with open arms. He would always ask at each visit, "How's the station doing?" I would always tell him fine, whether it was or not. The intent was not to lie to him, but I felt my answer to his question was relevant to the question and his definition of "doing." I knew he was a very astute businessman and my qualifications in the business world were somewhat less than his, to the point of being non-existent. I didn't know how a businessman judged success, and I was not about to guess. I didn't want him to feel like I carried a negative attitude about the ministry.

On this particular evening when Jane and I walked into his home, he asked the same question, "How's the radio station?" I gave my usual unrehearsed answer, "Fine." Jane, in her unassuming and direct manner, said, "If you don't tell him the truth, I will." I frantically shook my head no. Mr. Hodge didn't see me. He was looking at her as if to say, "What do you mean?" Before anyone could say anything Jane said, "It is doing terrible." "What do you mean terrible?" was his reply. "Tell him Ed how things are going." I looked at Jane as if to say, "You tell him. You started this. I didn't." I took a deep breath, waited a moment to collect my thoughts and told him exactly what was wrong. I shared the fact the money wasn't coming in to sustain the station, and I simply didn't know what to do. I was sitting on several thousand dollars of unpaid bills including the rent and other vital bills. He could see the anguish in my spirit and said, "Ed, if the people aren't going to support the station, shut the thing down." I sat there a few moments with thoughts racing through my

114

mind. "Is God finished? Is this the businessman or the friend or the father in him speaking trying to protect me? Does he really believe it's over?" I sat there speechless at his reaction. In a few moments he looked at Mary Eliza and nodded his head. She walked over to where I was sitting and handed me a folded check. As I started to put it in my shirt pocket, Mr. Hodge said, "Maybe this will help, go ahead and look at it." I felt pure love coming through his voice as I began to slowly unfold the check, not really knowing what to expect. "Oh my God," I practically yelled in his home. I handed the check to Jane and began to sob uncontrollably. Jane began to cry as she looked at the check in the amount of $25,000. In a flash of time I saw all the times of doubt, questioning God about the ministry, even walking in doubt. All I could say was, "God, please forgive me, and Mr. Hodge, thank you." Over and over that was all I could do, "Thank God and thank you." I was a happy but broken individual. We left his home that evening with joy, not despair, in our hearts thanking God for all He had done. I went to the station the next day, paid all the unpaid bills, and now had a surplus. It made for a good, relaxed Christmas.

Over the next several years Mr. Hodge generously gave to the ministry several times. It was always at a time when financially all was not good. It was as if God would say to him, "They need your help, now is the time." Mr. Hodge never tried to influence the way I was running the station and he was always there if I had questions or needed advice concerning the business side of the operation. He was a God-placed man at a God-given time to help a God-called ministry keep its head above water and survive the beginning years of its youth.

Mr. Hodge is now with the Lord. I know he is healed from all his diseases and the tears of his broken heart have been wiped from his eyes. The reward he received for helping not only WCCV but also individuals and ministries over this country must have been great. There is coming a day when Jane and I can once again see him and speak to him. I am looking forward to that moment. I believe my first words will go something like this, "Thank you for saving a ministry that has since seen thousands come to Christ, lives touched, and people healed." At the same time, if it hasn't already happened, he will simply be told, "Thank you for giving to the Lord." Over the years I have often thought about him. Without a second thought it is as if I am talking to him directly and a simple, thank you, will quietly emanate from my heart to him even though I know he is with the Lord. I think about the song recorded by Ray Boltz, *Thank You,* which says, "Thank you for giving to the Lord." Truly this man gave to the Lord.

In the meantime WCCV continued to broadcast the gospel. By now we were on the air from 6 a.m. until 11 p.m. I had hired a couple more staff, plus Jane and I were working between our regular jobs, her at the Cartersville Church of God as secretary and I at the Post Office. I would pinch the ministry's pennies until there was nothing left to pinch, but we seemed to never catch up. If we did it didn't stay that way because bills were always coming in the mail needing to be paid. The listeners didn't understand our support came from them and not the business community. Listeners were not accustomed to non-profit, non-commercial radio. The churches and main line denominations thought the Cartersville Church of God had funded, built and was operating the station and they would not get involved. A definite training and understanding was needed for the people, churches, and businesses, but the question was "how?" What were we supposed to do in the meantime?

At one particular time our finances were so bad that payroll being due in a couple of days was out of the question. I was in a quandary as to what needed to be done. As always in these situations, I would pray asking God for help. Sometimes He would answer and sometimes He would not. I'm sure everyone has experienced the same thing resulting from prayer. This time He answered the next morning, which was Thursday. The payroll was due Friday. I was praying, "God, your Word says a laborer is worthy of his hire. These people have been working in Your field, planting seeds, and doing work for Your Kingdom, and I have no way to give them their hire." He immediately responded with, "ASK AND YOU SHALL RECEIVE." I knew by the Spirit what He was saying. He wasn't saying to call people and ask or even ask Him, He was saying ask on the air for people to get involved in His work. I immediately instructed Wayne to let people know what our situation was, hiding nothing. The phones began to ring and people began coming into the station to bring money. The parade of assistance continued until the day was over. The next morning it began again although we had discontinued asking over the air. By the end of the second day enough money had come in not only for the payroll but also to catch up on all the bills.

I had seen a glimpse of revelation. Let people know. Let the Christian community know of your problem, and help will come either by God's direct intervention or by the hand of a few faithful to Him. The following week I was watching The 700 Club on the Christian Broadcasting

Network and they were conducting a fundraising event for their ministry, and suddenly I realized this is what God was talking about. Ask and you will receive. Not just once but when needed. Out of this encounter with reality and God, our Share Times were born.

The first Share Time we had was a springtime event and our budget was $4,000 for one month's operation. I set the date, announced it, and the first Spring Share was under way. It was scheduled to last five days beginning on Monday. Jane and I had taken off from work that week so we could take part in what I thought was going to be an eventful time of fundraising. We along with Wayne and Vince spent countless hours explaining public supported radio and why we were not allowed to sell commercials. We spent many hours sharing the Word of God and praying with and for people. The first pledge or offer of financial support was yet to be received. This went on from 6 a.m. until 11 p.m. each day. Monday, Tuesday, Wednesday, and Thursday passed with nothing, not the first pledge of financial support. I was discouraged. Did I really hear from God or was all of this my zeal? Why is this happening?

Jane in her beautiful personality kept reassuring me all was going to be fine. God would see us through. Friday, the last day, we continued to plug away asking, asking, asking and we kept on asking. Then I realized that was what the scripture meant. Don't just ask once but keep on asking until you receive. We endured. The final hour, previously scheduled to be 6 p.m. Friday, was rapidly approaching. As that hour approached and not one red cent pledged, I was very frustrated, not to mention aggravated. "Why don't they understand?" "Why don't they care?" These were some of the thoughts in my mind concerning the people, the listeners, as the closing moments of Spring Share steadily approached. Jane and I were standing near the desk in the lobby and suddenly the phone rang. I answered and the individual on the other end said, "Ed, I want to pledge $1,000 toward the ministry." I was ecstatic. I was so nervous I could hardly write his name and address down, not to mention talking to him. I thanked him over and over for his pledge which, by the way, was given to me at church the following Sunday. Spring Share had now come to a close. Was it successful? Financially, no it wasn't. Spiritually and academically, yes it was. We had all learned a great deal about fundraising and trusting God. In spite of all the disappointments during this fundraising event, He proved He was still there and still on the throne. Although we only raised 25% of what was needed to operate this ministry, God somehow got us through each succeeding day, week, and month maintaining the station in spite of my continuing doubts and fears. I was still learning and those lessons didn't come easy.

Share Time events continue to this day much the same as they were in the beginning. The budget is of course bigger, the staff is larger, and the ministry continues to grow with the hand of God directing it each step of the way. Of course there was then as there is now those that have the answers as to how every dollar should be raised and spent. People have accused us of begging. They would say, "Have faith and God will meet your need." I learned not to care what people thought. God had given me a vision to begin and a command to fulfill. I was the one responsible, not them. The comments of criticism started the day we signed on and never stopped. We, including myself, learned that everyone could not be pleased. Jesus didn't accomplish that task and we certainly didn't have the edge on perfection. During prayer one evening the Lord let me know He was in charge and not to listen to people and their ideas, especially if they were in direct contradiction to His instructions. If I did they would literally destroy the ministry that He had big plans for in the future. This included everyone, no exceptions. I developed a policy that I would listen politely to all, test the spirit, and compare it to what I knew in my heart God wanted. If it passed the test then I would act upon it. If it did not pass the test, I would discard it completely as flesh and not God. As always mistakes were made when misinterpretations took place on my part, but God in His abundant grace and mercy took care of every situation.

Chapter 10
Increasing Power... The Enemy Attacks

After a few months on the air, we continued to struggle financially as a ministry and I struggled with the ministry as a whole, wanting to make sure at all times we were not stepping into our own will and leaving God's will. We were still operating at the original 100 watts. I knew that we needed to increase our power for two reasons. One, we would be able to reach more people with the gospel, and two, it would as a result increase our financial base. I knew as the ministry grew we would need financial increase to broaden our boarders as God had instructed us to do. Our financial situation wasn't able to handle the enormous expense necessary to file an application, have an antenna built, and buy the necessary equipment needed to increase the power of a radio station. I talked to Steve, our engineer, about a possible power increase. He said he would be able to prepare and file an application saving us a great deal of money. This was a tremendous break.

Steve was a very busy man with his regular job. It took him several months to complete the application. One evening he called me and said, "Ed, we can't put in the 3,000 watts as we expected." "Why?" I asked. He replied that a station in Cumming, Georgia had applied for a power increase and their coverage area would come very close to our existing one. Therefore, we could only apply for 910 watts using a directional antenna. My spirit sank to the floor. "Is that all we can do?" I asked. "I'm afraid so," he replied. I was sick at my stomach, not at the other station because they were a Christian station and needed to reach as far as they could to bring the gospel to the radio audience. I was sick because I now fully realized the mistake I made in the very beginning when I authorized the consulting engineer to file for 100 watts because it would cost less money to build. Neither he nor I ever dreamed we would be blocked in trying to increase to 3000 watts at a later date. The 3000 watts would have put our signal into Marietta, Woodstock, Powder Springs, and Northwest Atlanta without the use of translators. Everyone would have been able to receive WCCV at 91.7 FM and not different frequencies. "What have I done?" Over and over I asked myself that question. "Why didn't I have enough faith to believe God for just a little extra?" I was almost tormented with these thoughts. I realized I had to get myself, along with my thoughts, back in line. I could not change the situation, and I certainly could not change the FCC rules regarding interference of one station to another.

I finally told Steve to prepare and file the application with the FCC. In March 1984, the application was filed and the waiting process began. I knew it would take eight or nine months at least to process, so I began working as best I could on what this project would cost. Directional antennas are very expensive. A directional antenna is designed to send less signal strength in the direction of a station you would interfere with if your signal were at full strength. The mechanics of accomplishing this is time consuming and detailed for the manufacturer. All parameters must be in exact accordance with FCC specifications and the application filed. It must be mounted on the tower and pointed in a certain direction verified by a surveyor. In addition, a new transmitter would be needed because of the increased power. I could see dollar signs beginning to add up the ministry didn't have. God said to broaden our borders, so I had to believe He would somehow supply what was needed to meet this next vital and important step in the life of this ministry.

During the first few months of 1984, the uncertainty of absolute direction, the continuous financial strain, the tremendous stress created by the newness of the ministry, along with the fairly new postal job, was taking its toll on me. My strength, my faith, and the vision God had given me appeared to be waning. It is so easy to forget the miraculous days of the past when the present isn't going the way we want it to. I was beginning to doubt God's assurance to supply the needs and direction of the ministry. I was constantly frustrated, and yes, I worried a great deal. My attitude began to take on negative thoughts, actions, and words. I seemed to be in a never-ending downward spiral completely unable to stop what was happening. Knowing I had a very serious spiritual problem that seemed to be getting worse with each passing day, I determined in my heart to find an answer. I did not know at the time God was preparing me to learn a very important, valuable spiritual lesson. He was going to teach me this in a powerful way during the weeks and days ahead through the power of His Holy Spirit.

In February during a church revival service, I committed myself to two hours of Bible reading and prayer each night before going to bed. I set the time each evening 7 to 9 p.m. Nothing was to interfere with this time alone with God. The place was my bedroom, door closed with instructions not to disturb me unless an emergency arose. I would lie on the floor night after night reading scripture and seeking God for answers.

During this time I was working full-time at the post office. My working hours were from 4:30 a.m. to 1:30 p.m. with a lunch hour from 11:30 to 12:30. Having to work at the post office to make a living for my family and trying to keep abreast of everything at the radio station, making decisions, and answering questions was a monumental task. At the time I had no choice, because Jane and I were not drawing a paycheck from the ministry.

I would go to the station on my lunch hour each day to take care of the business of the ministry and answer any questions that needed to be handled. My staff was very capable and trustworthy but my heart was still at the station and not at the post office. My wife Jane, my daughter Denise, and my son-in-law Brian Barnette were always there and I didn't worry about the day-to-day operation. They were very capable, but I was still responsible, and I strongly felt this responsibility.

One day in early March 1984, I was on my lunch hour, not in the best of moods and had a bad attitude. I went to my desk at the radio station as usual to see if I had any messages. Lying there was the cash report I had Jane prepare for me each day so I could keep a handle on our financial situation at all times. The report was terrible. Very little of the money pledged, promised, or committed by the listeners during our last Share Time was coming in. A mountain of bills had accumulated and needed to be paid. The people we owed for their services wanted their money, and we had no resource to get any. This was an ongoing problem, and this particular day I was at my wit's end. I got very angry, picked up the report, and slammed it down on my desk, yelling at the top of my voice, "This is God's fault!!!" I sat down, sulking and pouting as if that was going to move God's heart or change His mind. I went back to work at the post office, finished my day, and went home very disgusted. However, after a few days, I didn't really think about my explosion in the office anymore. It became just an incident that to me was better forgotten about.

I noticed while sorting mail at the post office each morning, sitting quietly alone on my mail-sorting stool, I would hear thoughts that very rapidly began to trouble me. These thoughts would be quietly spoken but very profound voices. They sounded like my voice sounds to me when I talk. It was as if I was "strongly" thinking, if there was such a thing. These thoughts would say things like, "You are not a leader. You aren't qualified to run this so-called ministry. This ministry was your idea not God's. Why don't you quit? You aren't worthy for God to call you to do anything. This radio station is going to fail, and it is your fault. The finances are in the shape they are in because of your inability to manage money. You are not a businessman. You have failed, go ahead and admit it." On and on it would go. I would hear thoughts that would accuse the employees, by name more often than not, of doing things behind my back and trying to take over the station by planting bad thoughts and ideas in the minds of other employees to discredit me.

This went on for weeks. Weeks became months. It was a never-ending barrage of accusations and fault-finding. I was absolutely tormented by this constant badgering and thoughts. I was an individual without much self-esteem and almost no self-confidence. I have always thought lowly about myself and about my abilities to accomplish anything. Consequently, I have always taken criticism, whether constructive or otherwise, personally, as a reflection of that inability. This onslaught of "thoughts" wasn't helping any. After a while I noticed when leaving the post office and going to the station or home the voices would stop. I really began to question my sanity. As time went by the voices and accusations became stronger and more obnoxious. It would only happen while working at the post office, and on a rare occasion, at home on the weekends, but never at the radio station.

I continued to pray each night, rebuking the devil, asking God for help and nothing seemed to work. One evening I was desperately, fervently crying out to for help. "What do you want me to do?" was my prayer. Time after time that night I would ask the same question. I had no answers and wasn't getting any answers. "Why...Why? Help me." I truly began to feel the voice I was hearing at the post office was the Lord because I wasn't hearing, feeling, or sensing anything else. I got very upset and was about to quit praying for the evening, and I thought I would try one more time. "What do you want me to do?" As soon as the last word crossed my lips, I heard in a very gruff, low, grizzly, authoritative sounding voice, "Resign." I cried out, "No...No, you can't mean that. Please Lord, don't make me resign." The silence was deafening. I got up and went to Jane in tears. I said, "Jane, when the Lord speaks to you how does it sound?" She said, "It is always a sweet, loving, caring voice." I told her what had just happened and how it sounded. She said, "No, that was not God. I believe it was the devil trying to stop you from fulfilling God's calling on your life. Just forget it." I felt very comfortable with that. I guess I truly wanted her to be right, so I continued my nightly prayers and seeking God for answers. That type of incident never happened again. I was, however, still having problems hearing from God.

One Monday while at the station during a Share Time, I said something on the air that displayed my anger and frustration. Later that morning Terry Elrod, a Board of Directors member, came to the station and asked if he could go into the prayer room and pray for a while. I, of course said yes, without any further conversation. After a few minutes he called me into the prayer room and asked if he could pray with me. I allowed it as always. Prayer was always welcome.

We kneeled on the floor, held hands and began praying. After a few words, Terry looked up at me and said, "I need to talk to you." We got up off the floor and he sat in the chair and I sat on the prayer bench. He looked at me and said, "Brother Ed, I saw something, but I don't know how to tell you what it was." I said, "Just say it brother, I need all the help I can get." He said, "Okay, here goes. I saw a demon attached to you. It was right behind your ear and whispering to you." My response, sarcastic of course, was, "Great, what do I do about that?" He said, "My pastor has a deliverance ministry. I will call him." Terry got his pastor on the phone and told him what had happened when he prayed for me. I knew the pastor. He was a very private, humble person. He asked to speak to me. I took the phone. He said, "Ed, I heard you on the air earlier and from what Terry tells me and from what I have heard, you need a deliverance." I said, "Okay, what do I do?" After talking a few moments, we made an appointment to meet in the basement of his church the following Thursday at 7 p.m.

I had absolutely no idea what was going to happen. I wasn't really sure what a deliverance consisted of. Neither

Jane nor I had ever been taught about demons, their power, or what they could do, especially to Christians. We knew about them and the fact they existed. We knew about satan and his role in this world. We knew he came to kill, steal, and destroy, but I never related that to me personally or to Christianity in general. I had never really given that particular scripture much thought. I assumed it was talking about the world and the situations people and nations find themselves.

Though I greatly anticipated the meeting, I was anxious and also apprehensive. Thursday evening finally arrived. Jane and I went, as directed, to the church basement. Upon arriving, the pastor, another man from the church, whom I didn't know, and Terry were waiting for us. Jane and I were introduced to the gentleman who was one of the spiritual leaders of the church. Terry and the other gentleman excused themselves momentarily to tend to some church business and went upstairs.

The pastor asked me into his office while Jane remained in the other room. He asked me several questions. He asked what was happening and how I felt. I tried to explain the best I could, all the time fumbling for words because my situation and frame of mind was very difficult to explain to anyone. In his God given wisdom, he understood my ramblings and said, "Ed, satan doesn't like that radio station because it is a very real threat to him. He knows it has a future, and he is going to try and stop it. He knows if he can stop you, he can destroy the ministry. He is fully aware you were called to build it and that you are the leader." He asked if I understood, and I told him I did. During this time, Jane was in the other room praying for me, the situation, and what was about to happen. He asked Jane to come into the office. He asked her only one question.

While she was in his office, I sat at a table and opened my bible and began reading. I was in the book of Isaiah, chapter 38. I read a few minutes, not really having my mind on the Bible but on the events about to transpire, of which I was completely ignorant. I was only reading words and not particularly focused, when suddenly these words leaped off the page, as if they were written in bold, black lettering. "I WILL DELIVER THEE." I couldn't believe my eyes. I collected my thoughts, looked at the scripture again. I was in verse six. I read those four words over and over again. They were the only words in the entire verse that spoke to me. As I read them repeatedly, I could hear a still small voice inside me saying, "TONIGHT."

When he and Jane left his office, all of us gathered in an open area in the basement of the church. The pastor said, "Ed, I don't want you to do one thing but sit in this chair. We will do it all." He prayed protection around us, around our homes and our families. He then said to the others, "Ed is oppressed by at least one demon that has attached itself to him and is tormenting him in an attempt to destroy him and the ministry. It is our job to pray a prayer of deliverance in the name of Jesus, commanding the demon to leave him and go to the pit from where it came. We must be in agreement and we must be sensitive. Ed, you do anything you feel like doing. If it is running, jumping, screaming, vomiting, coughing, or whatever, you do it. Pay no attention to us and do not let us hinder you. Are each of you ready?"

They began praying fervently for the demon to leave me and go to the pit in Jesus' name. They were praying with authority in the Spirit and in English. This went on for a few minutes, and I, of course, felt nothing. I wasn't really sure what I was supposed to feel or what was going to happen. I had already forgotten the scripture just moments earlier that seemed to jump off the page about being delivered.

Suddenly, the pastor said, "Stop. God has shown me that you, Ed, have angrily accused Him of something, and He wants you to ask for His forgiveness and repent." I immediately thought of the day in my office when I threw the cash report down on my desk putting the blame on God for the financial problem at the station. How could the pastor know except God had told him, because Jane had not spoken a word of this to him. Jane and I were the only ones that even knew we had a problem at the station, not to mention how I showed my temper that day. I was amazed, but at the same time humbled to the point I began to weep. I asked God to forgive me for what I had done, and I promised I would never do it again. The pastor said, "Now that is taken care of, let's proceed."

They all began praying again in that authoritative manner while I just sat there taking God at His Word that I had been forgiven. After what seemed like an hour but was only a few minutes, I began feeling a tickling in my throat. It was as if I needed to clear it, but couldn't. Attempting to clear my throat again and again, the pastor instructed me to try harder. I didn't know what was happening except I had a tickle in my throat. Praying, they got louder and more authoritative. This went on for several minutes. I was sitting and not saying a word. Just clearing my throat.

All of a sudden, I heard a voice that sounded like my voice. The same voice I would hear while working at the post office. It was to my right a little further away from me than the length of my arm stretched out. It said, "I'll be back." It startled me because I certainly wasn't prepared to hear voices coming out of the air. I told the pastor what I heard. He said very loudly speaking in the direction of the voice I had heard, "No you won't. You are a liar." I said, "What was that?" The pastor said, "That was the demon that has been tormenting you at work and at other times. You thought it was you thinking all this time. You weren't. It was a demon of torment imitating your voice and speaking all of those accusations and demeaning statements to you. It is gone. Now let's pray and see if there are more before we leave."

After a few more minutes of praying the pastor said, "There is another one. It is a demon of worry." They began praying against it. I felt nothing and heard or sensed nothing. As a matter of fact this wasn't too bad. I was ready to rid myself of all demonic influence if it would make me happier and enjoy life more. As they continued praying, the pastor said, "There it goes. The demon of worry is gone." I felt absolutely nothing. I said to myself, if he knew I said what I said in my office that day, certainly he knows what he is talking about now. I just took him at his word. If he said it is gone, then it is gone. He said, "Let's continue to pray and see if there are more."

They prayed for what seemed like thirty minutes. Terry, standing behind me spoke up and said, "I see another one. This one is a big one. It has tentacles entwined all through Ed's body like a large octopus. It has been there for a long time. It is a demon of anger." They began commanding, praying, speaking, and demanding in Jesus' name for that demon to release me. The pastor asked if there was anything in my childhood that could have allowed such a demon as this to attach itself to me. I knew immediately of a number of things that transpired in my youth, but I wasn't at liberty to speak of them. He said, "You don't have to tell us. I wanted you to know you have had this one since you were a child."

They continued praying and after what seemed like an hour the pastor said, "Here it comes. Keep it up. This is a tough one because it is so deep rooted after having been there so long." They continued to pray and speak directly to the demon to leave me and go to the pit. They said, "He has had a comfortable home for so long that he doesn't want to leave but he has no choice. He has to obey when Jesus' name is used. He knows Jesus and was probably there when He was crucified, so the demon knows with whom he is dealing."

Without me having any indication, the pastor spoke and said, "It is gone. I saw it leave." I was completely unaware of this one leaving, but that didn't matter to me. I was willing to take his word. The pastor said, "He is clean there are no more. Ed has been swept clean and except he be filled with God's Holy Spirit, the demons will come back seven times worse." I said, "None of that. Let's pray for the house to be filled." The pastor spoke up and said, "Okay Ed, stand up, raise your hands to heaven. We are going to lay hands on you and ask for Jesus to fill you to overflowing." I did as he instructed but nothing happened. I wanted a manifestation so I could say I know that I know that I know. The Pastor spoke up and said, "Wait a minute." I thought, "Oh, No! Here we go again. Something else I've done that I need to ask forgiveness for and repent." He continued speaking, "Ed, you have built a wall around yourself. It is like a circle around you and domed at the top to even cover your head. It is made out of cement block and has to be removed. It is interfering with your communication with God and everyone else. Here is what I want you to do. Since this is a spiritual matter, I want you to close your eyes and imagine the domed cylinder that covers you. I want you to begin, in your mind, to remove that dome one block at the time until it is all removed. Go ahead and start now."

I did as he asked. I closed my eyes imagining the dome over me. I could almost see it. In my mind, I began removing the blocks as he instructed, one at a time very slow and methodical. Jane, the Pastor, Terry, and the other gentleman were very quiet. I guess they were tired from all the laborious and difficult intercession of the past few hours. After several minutes of removing blocks, the pastor asked, "How far are you?" I replied, "Down to my knees." He said, "Go ahead and step out if you can and rid yourself of that wall." I literally took a high step as if I was stepping over a wall about knee high. Then I brought the other foot out. When the second foot touched the floor outside the dome, all of heaven opened up. It was as if God had split the heavens and began pouring love all over me. It was a continuous flow from the throne to me. I knew it was just for me. I fell to my knees and began to worship my God that had fulfilled His word the same night He spoke to me out of Isaiah, "I WILL DELIVER THEE." I don't know how long this went on. Although I had to be at work at 4:30 a.m., the time didn't matter even though it was almost 11:00 p.m. We finally calmed down and prepared to leave the church. We hugged each other and I couldn't thank them enough for spending their evening praying for me. They actually cared about me and cared about my relationship with God. There aren't many people like them anymore.

Jane and I started the drive home. I felt so light and carefree. It was remarkable. A car coming toward us on the other side of the road had its bright lights on. I flashed mine as one always does so the other driver would dim his. He didn't, so I just put mine on bright and said, "Here buddy, take that." At the moment I did, God spoke to me, "YOU SHOULDN'T HAVE DONE THAT." I had, at that moment, heard the voice of God in a way I had not heard it in a long, long time. It was glorious. Words are inadequate to describe the sound of His voice and the peace it produced within my soul. I said, "I'm sorry." I dimmed my lights. The other car passed me going the other way never dimming his and it didn't bother me at all.

We arrived home after midnight. I knew 3:30 a.m. was going to be early. We went to bed, and I must say in those few hours I had the most restful sleep in what seemed like years. When the clock alarmed, I got up as if I had eight hours sleep and felt wonderful. I had not been able to say that very often since called to build the radio station.

I got to work at the post office the next morning feeling good, refreshed, and ready to go to work. I sat down on my stool and began sorting the mail. Suddenly I realized, no voices. There were none of those tormenting voices and degrading statements. I had been fully delivered and set free from the power of hell. I was absolutely ecstatic. I tried to think of some of the things I would hear while working. I couldn't even bring them to my mind. I was one happy man and forever grateful to

Jesus for answering my prayers and the prayers of the saints that prayed for me that memorable Thursday night in the basement of the house of God. I had been delivered in His Name, the Name of Jesus.

Why didn't someone tell me demons could and would torment Christians? Why didn't someone teach on demonic activity so we as the body of Christ would be aware of his devices? Jane and I studied everything we could find about the subject so we would not be caught off guard again. The theology going around that demons don't bother Christians is straight from the pits of hell. It is a doctrine of demons, spoken by the demons themselves so they will have the upper hand trying to accomplish the task they are assigned. That is to steal, kill, and destroy. They almost accomplished that with me.

As the days passed I could not believe my state of mind. It was impossible for me to think an impure thought. It was as if my heart and mind had been washed to think and receive only holiness. Pure thoughts, pure motives, pure and complete love was all I knew. It was as if I understood how Jesus lived on this earth 33 ½ years without sin. I felt as if I had a small taste of that purity and holiness in which He lived.

This spiritual euphoria continued for about ten days. One afternoon, after getting home from work at the post office, I lay down on the bed to take a nap. After all 3:30 a.m. was very early in the morning. An occasional nap was necessary because the flesh was still weak regardless of the spiritual strength I had been experiencing.

In what seemed like moments but was actually about an hour, there was a knock at the front door. It awakened me and really aggravated me because I didn't lay down often in the afternoon but this time I was really tired. I went to the front door. Standing there was two guys dressed in white shirts with ties wanting to talk to me about their religion and telling me all about Jesus being seen in South America. I listened for about ten seconds. I was furious. I grabbed the edge of the front door, screamed at them, "I don't want to hear anything you have to say!!!" I slammed the front door in their face, turned around, and started back to bed. I did not get there.

My insides were jerking like I was going to have a seizure. There was anger boiling up in my gut. I was ready to fight. I am not a fighter. I have never been in a fight in my entire life, except with my brother, but this day I was ready to almost kill. The rage boiling in me was absolutely unbelievable. It was totally uncontrollable. In a few minutes Jane came home from work. She asked me what I wanted for supper, and I almost yelled at her, "I don't know and I don't care."

I went to the front bedroom to be alone and try to figure out through the rage and anger what was wrong with me. My inside felt like a different person was present trying to get out and that person was not pleasant. The anger, the absolute rage within me was something I had never encountered. I didn't know how to deal with it. I felt as if I could put my fist through a wall or a door, I would feel better. I didn't, but I sure wanted to.

Shortly Jane called me for supper. I was a raving maniac inside and really didn't care who knew it. Jane asked me to call Howard for supper. He was next door playing basketball on the neighbor's basketball court. I could see him from our dining room window. I opened the window and screamed as if he was a mile away, "Howard, get in this house for supper!!!!" Jane said, "You didn't have to do it like that." I retorted with, "I'll do it any way I want to."

About this time Howard came into the house and said as kind and gentle as anyone could be, "Daddy, what is wrong?" I yelled back at him, "Nothing, leave me alone." Jane said, "You need to get control of yourself. What is going on?" I didn't respond. I finished my supper, got up from the table, and said, "I am going to the front bedroom to see if I can figure out what is wrong. I don't want anyone to bother me."

Just 24 hours earlier I was basking in the holiness, peace and love of Jesus, and here I am now acting like a proverbial fool. I closed the door behind me and got down on my knees still raging inside. I cried out to God. "What is wrong with me? Help me God? What have I done to cause this anger and rage. Oh God, send the angels to minister to me. I need help. Please God, please. I can't live like this. I won't live like this. This is horrible." On and on my pleas for help were voiced to the Lord. I wasn't sure if He was even listening, but I kept trying.

After about 30 minutes, I got up and went to bed. I was still angry and still raging, like my insides were going to spill out of me. I wasn't sure I could even go to sleep, but I went to bed anyhow. I wasn't any good to myself and certainly wasn't any good to my family, whom I had verbally abused as far as I was concerned. I went to sleep immediately.

At approximately 2 a.m. I awoke to these words, "God is love...God is love." Over and over I kept feeling and hearing those words. I looked to see if Jane was awake and talking to me, she wasn't. I could feel around my heart area a sensation of "little beings" moving around. It felt as if each had a hammer and chisel chiseling what

137

seemed to be stone and throwing the pieces out of me into space. Each strike of the hammer would remove a small piece of stone and with each strike I would hear, "God is love...God is love." I wasn't dreaming. Something was taking place in the spiritual realm. This continued for about a minute, and I was, by now, fully awake experiencing this phenomenon as realistically as any one could experience anything. Suddenly the last hammer blow was given, and I felt all the love, holiness, and purity fill my soul as it did that evening in the basement of the church. What had happened? I did not know, but something invaded my spirit earlier causing the anger, making a different person out of me, much different than my normal character would dictate.

I got up at the usual 3:30 a.m., got ready, and went to work. I was fine now. It was as if none of the rage and anger had happened. I was floating again. After the workload diminished a little I was thinking over the events of the last 12 hours and really wanted to talk to someone about what had happened. One of the clerks, Charles Reece, was an avid Christian and regular church attendee. He had an open mind about spiritual matters so I shared everything from the deliverance to the events of the last evening into this morning. I felt he was the only one that would come close to understanding.

He listened politely, waited for a moment and said, "Ed, I think you had an encounter with a demon of deception. It came when those two guys came to your front door. You were in a situation that angered you plus you had been on such a spiritual high that your guard was down. When you opened the door, the demon that accompanied them saw fresh meat and jumped on you immediately resulting in the rage and anger. It wasn't you

138

or your personality that was in that condition, it was the demon that attacked you acting like its normal self, trying to steal, kill, and/or destroy you." That sounded logical, so I accepted Charlie's explanation and felt good about it.

Jane was not aware I had experienced another deliverance because she was asleep when it happened, and I didn't awaken her. This time it happened in my bed, not in the church and was accomplished by the angels of God, not the efforts of man. She called about 7:00 a.m. very solemn and crying. She asked how I was doing and I told her I was fine. She went on to say, "I was praying for you this morning and the Lord told me that a demon of deception had attacked you and that was why you had acted the way you did. It wasn't really you but the demon." Before she could go any further I interrupted her saying, "Honey, it is all over. Please forgive me." I told her what Charlie had shared with me, confirming what she knew the Lord had spoken to her that morning. When I got home that evening I apologized to Howard and all was back to normal at the Tuten household. I had learned another valuable lesson. That lesson was simply our armor must be on at all times, because the devil can and will attack at any vulnerable or weak spot. He will do so with destruction as his goal.

In December 1984, the FCC issued us a permit to construct and implement the power increase. Eighteen months were allotted for the completion of the project. I began praying and seeking God. I could see it happening all over again as in the beginning. I desperately sought ways to raise money for this project. With the exception of going on the air and asking, I had no other choices. I couldn't do as churches or evangelists do and pass the offering plate requesting funds for a specific purpose. I couldn't conduct large crusades and have thousands of dollars put in the coffers of the ministry. All we could do was share the plight on the air without conducting a fundraiser. Would people listen? Would people understand? Would people realize we were not trying to fill our pockets but literally do something for them and the cause of Christ? Over the course of months, several thousand dollars came in from asking on the air, but that was not nearly enough. It was all we could do to keep our head above water just paying operating expenses, not to mention adding another expense to the ledger.

The problem was the people who would be affected by a power increase couldn't hear the station, and the people that could hear it didn't need a power increase. Time was quickly passing, and the 18 months were coming much faster than I needed them to. If the increase wasn't implemented in that given time, the permit was void and the process would have to be started over again. I was getting frantic. Again letting my flesh get in the way of God and certainly not using faith. Jane kept encouraging me as she always did, "Honey, God is going to take care of it." All I could see was reality. Faith was not in my make-up at the moment.

The deadline was July 23, 1986. It was now June. I knew there was nothing more I could do. The people were praying for us, but the money just wasn't there. One evening in late June, Fred Harris called me at home. He talked to Jane a few minutes and I heard her say, "Fred, you need to talk to Ed about that." She gave me the phone and we talked a few moments. Fred asked about the power increase and where we stood in getting it implemented. I shared with him it was going to cost $39,000 including the $2,000 we already had. He said to me, "Ed, I don't have that kind of money, but I have made some arrangements with the bank. I want you to go to the First National Bank tomorrow, tell them who you are, and they will take care of the rest. I have cosigned a note for what you need. Tell them what it is, and they will then give you the money to increase your power."

After thanking him over and over I hung up the phone, grabbed Jane and hugged her, crying the whole time. I told her what had just happened and we just stood there in each other's arms sobbing in thanksgiving for what God had done. Once again I saw the weakness of my faith and the strength of my flesh. God was all the time trying to show me He was in control, and my fretting did no good at all. I was gradually learning the faith walk, but it was very, very difficult for me. Jane on the other hand was full of faith and full of God. I believe God did this to not only bless her but to keep me on the straight and narrow, the way of His path. Had both of us been doubters and fretters, WCCV would have first never gotten on the air and secondly, never increased power.

I notified Steve that evening, telling him we had the money and we could get started. He immediately filed for an extension to the July 23 deadline and the orders went out for the antenna, transmitter, and microwave unit. For the first time since signing on the air a few years earlier, WCCV was now in debt. I didn't particularly like being in debt, but I believe God opened a door to accomplish His mission, and I wasn't about to allow that door to close without at least giving it a try. Little did I know the stage was set by Him to perform a miracle where only He could get the glory, but also to bless Jane, myself, the staff, and a multitude of people a couple of years in the future.

The FCC approved a six-month extension and the equipment began to arrive. Steve went to work immediately. On September 29, 1986, at 6:00 p.m., we turned off the old and turned on the new. We had been talking about it on the air so people knew what was going on. Shortly, we began getting reports from cities such as Rome, Adairsville, Calhoun, Dallas, and other cities we had never heard from. It was very exciting. At least it was for Jane and me. We shared on the air what God had done to get us to this point. We praised and honored Him all evening. We couldn't seem to praise Him enough.

A few days later stark reality again stared me in the face. "How am I going to pay this back to the bank?" I discussed it with the Board of Directors and some of the staff including Jane. We decided to wait a year to 18 months and have a special Share Time just for the loan. We felt at that time we would have picked up enough listeners in our new listing area that maybe we could do this.

About a year later we decided to start the process of trying to pay the bank back the principle and not just pay interest. We scheduled a Thursday, Friday, and Saturday in September 1987, and called it, for the lack of a better name, "Power Payback Days." For several weeks we had bombarded the airways with what we were going to do and we needed 370 people to give $100 each to pay off our debt. The money was needed as soon as possible so we could get the debt wiped out.

On the date preset Power Payback Days began. The phones began ringing and the people were coming to our aid. One hundred dollar pledges were pouring in as fast as we could take them. For three days this happened. People would come in off the street giving $5, $10, whatever they could to pay this debt off. Friday, the second day, was no different. The phones rang and the people came. It was the most amazing, exciting thing I had ever seen so far as fund raising was concerned. On Saturday, the same was taking place. The staff and volunteers had worked so hard, I decided that no matter what, we would shut it down at 11:00 p.m. As the evening approached, the phone calls and pledges began slowing down. There was a trickle here and there but nothing to completely finish the total needed. At approximately 9 p.m. we were $750 from the goal. It was miraculous. This little station, by the Grace of God, had raised almost $37,000 in three days, and now we were so close to finishing but not quite there. For 45 minutes there was not one phone call. Our hearts were literally aching at the possibility we would end at 11:00 and not complete the goal. At about 10:00 the phone rang. I answered and it was the husband of one of the staff that had been working endless, tiring hours since Power Payback Days had started three days before. He said, "Ed, how much do you need to finish?" I said, "$750." He replied, "If you will send my wife home, I'll give the $750."

I need not tell you about the shouts of jubilation and praise going forth from the radio station that evening. God had worked another miracle for WCCV and for the staff, continuing to show us that He was still in control. There must have been about 20 people standing around the studios that unforgettable evening. As the praise went forth from the station, the glory of God came down. I got on the air and tried in a feeble attempt to thank God for what He had done and thank the people for being so obedient to what God wanted.

As the money continued to come in, we applied 100% of the pledged money to the principle of the note. Eighteen months after taking out the loan, it was paid off in full and WCCV was once again out of debt. God in His mercy supplied the regular operating expense funds from His people in addition to the loan payoff money. It was a beautiful, memorable time in the life of the ministry.

Chapter 11
Shadow of Death

With the beautiful movement of God to pay off our debt, WCCV moved along fairly smooth for the next several months. I was always looking for ways to improve our coverage area with translators. Rome, the largest city in Northwest Georgia, did not receive the signal of WCCV clearly. I was trying everything I knew to get a better signal in that area, but our only solution was to build a translator because there were not any frequencies available for regular FM radio stations. I believe God in His omniscience had this planned, if for no other reason, to save my life because He wasn't finished with me.

Saturday, July 10, 1988, Jane and I attended Cedar Lake Christian Center in Cedartown, Georgia for their evening camp-meeting service. The praise and worship music was extraordinary. It was as if we were standing in the presence of God Almighty Himself. It was worship like I had not experienced in a long time.

As I was participating in the worship, I began to feel a little discomfort in the middle of my chest. I rubbed it a bit and kept singing with my hands held high. The discomfort didn't go away, but didn't get any worse. I thought to myself, "Well, I'm catching a summer cold," and tried to forget about it. The service continued to its conclusion. Jane and I left the church to return home to Cartersville. It is about a 45-minute drive from one city to the other. I told Jane I would drive home since she had a little difficulty driving at night. I felt fine and had not told her about the incident happening in church earlier that evening.

By the time we arrived home, the discomfort was a little more painful. I shared with Jane the feeling I was having and again put it off as being a summer cold. We went to bed and during the night, I awoke with more pain this time accompanied by a little pressure. I also had an uncomfortable feeling in my neck and in both arms. I couldn't attribute that to a cold, but neither did I attribute it to my heart or any other part of my body. I still thought, for the most part, I was catching a cold and that was why my chest was hurting and felt tight. The next day, Sunday, we attended church and had the pastor pray for me, because I really wasn't sure what was happening.

I went to bed Sunday night feeling better and immediately went to sleep. I awoke for my regular shift at the post office around 3:30 a.m. Monday morning. I felt fine. There was no pain and no pressure. It was as if the incidents of the previous two days had not happened. I thought God had healed me Sunday in church. I worked my shift, spent my usual time at the radio station, and went home about 4:00 p.m. I took a short nap. By the time I awoke, Jane was home from work and Howard was home from school.

I wasn't really doing anything, and sometime around 5 o'clock, I began to feel that discomfort again. I told Jane about it and again blamed it on catching a cold. As the next few minutes progressed, the discomfort in my chest began increasing, getting quite painful. There was tremendous pressure building up. I pushed back in the lounging chair and asked Jane to put a hot towel on my chest and take the ball of her hand and press on my chest to see if it would relieve any of the pressure. She did, all the time saying, "You need to call the doctor." I am saying, "All he will do is give me a shot for the cold I am getting." She continued to press on my chest. That would relieve the pain. I began thinking by now not only was I catching a cold, I had developed indigestion from something I had eaten earlier.

After about thirty minutes the pain began to subside, and I was feeling better. I wasn't tired, weak, or disoriented. I really felt good when my chest wasn't hurting. I continued to rest in the recliner and Jane asked what I wanted for supper. I told her to fix my favorite: two cheeseburgers and fries. She did and I ate all of it still never thinking anything was wrong with me. I slept well during the night with no problem.

On Tuesday, July 12, I had an appointment with the manager of the new television station in Rome. My purpose was to ask about WCCV using some space on their tower on Horseleg Mountain. I wanted to put up a translator station to rebroadcast the WCCV signal from Cartersville. This would give Rome better reception of WCCV from the translator station, but would require us putting an antenna on their tower. The manager told me he would have to contact their engineer and would let me know.

When we left the TV station on our way home to Cartersville, Jane said, "Ed, I don't like the pains you were having the other night. Why don't you go to the doctor while you are here in Rome?" At that time, my doctor was in Rome, and I always had to travel from Cartersville to Rome each time I needed to see him for any reason. I, of course, objected. She said, "It isn't far from here, why don't you go?" The next traffic light, which wasn't far from us, was where I would have to turn. A right turn would be home to Cartersville and a left turn would be the doctor's office. Jane was saying, "Please," and I was

147

contemplating. I still thought I was catching a cold and felt the trip to the doctor would have been an absolute waste of time.

At the last minute I said, "Okay, if it will make you feel any better." She said in her usual sweet way, "Thank you." I made the left turn and in a matter of minutes we were at the doctor's office. I just knew without an appointment we would be there half the day. I walked up to the counter, signed in, and sat down. In a few seconds the receptionist asked, "What is the reason for seeing the doctor? Since you don't have an appointment, we will have to work you in." I said, "I have been having some chest pains, but I feel like it is a cold. My wife insisted I come by here to see the doctor and be sure."

In no more than five minutes the nurse called me to the back. She put me in a room, took my vitals, and asked me to be seated. No sooner than she got the words out of her mouth, the doctor walked in. He asked me to explain what had been happening. I went over the events since Sunday evening at church and how I had pain and pressure in my chest at different times since then. He said, "I am going to do a electro-cardiogram to see if we can figure out what is going on."

The test complete, the doctor returned a few minutes later and said, "Ed, I have compared this electro-cardiogram with the one taken last year and there is a marked change between the two. I feel like this is serious enough to hospitalize you, run more tests, and see if we can determine what is happening."

I had no choice but to submit to his request because this was beginning to sound serious. This was the first time I even thought about the problem being my heart. My family had a history of heart trouble. I had been warned about my possible predisposition to the disease. My dad died at 55 and a number of his ten brothers and sisters died early because of heart conditions. It was prevalent on both sides of my family. I never thought it would happen to me, especially at 49 years of age. All the symptoms were there, but for some reason I refused, either consciously or subconsciously, to believe what I knew now my body was telling me. I had seen my dad go through similar pain before his heart attack at 45 years old. Why would I be any different with the same symptoms and practically the same age?

I was checked into Floyd Medical Center in Rome almost immediately and they wired me to a heart monitor, began taking blood, running tests, and scheduling different physical tests. Generally, heart patients, or suspect heart patients, were sent to Redmond Hospital across town from Floyd because that is where the cardiac unit was located. At this particular time there were no private rooms available at Redmond, so they checked me into Floyd.

The staff ran tests again Tuesday afternoon, and I heard nothing about the results. I began getting very impatient. My orders were to stay in bed. Only with the assistance of a nurse could I get out of bed. The doctor came in that evening but had no results. I was not pleased. I wasn't having any more chest problems and began complaining about wanting to go home.

I complained into Wednesday morning. I complained to the doctor and anyone else I could find. With each passing moment, I was more and more ready to leave that hospital and go home. I had a lot of work to do. I had a job at the post office to maintain, and I was too busy to be lying in bed doing absolutely nothing. I tossed and turned. I fussed and griped. I was almost ugly to the nurses. I saw no reason for keeping me there. I wasn't hurting, and I wasn't getting any reports from the tests, so I naturally assumed I was in good health. I was catching a cold as I said before. Surely if it was my heart, something would have shown up by now.

All of a sudden, out of nowhere, God spoke to me, "BE STILL. YOU ARE HERE FOR YOUR OWN GOOD." I froze in the bed. I was speechless. In a moment I told Jane what I had heard and was honestly afraid to open my mouth about anything. So for the duration of the day I was quiet and still, giving no one a problem.

Later that afternoon the doctor came in and said, "Ed, we need to talk. We have looked at all your tests and talked your situation over with some of the cardiologists on staff. We feel the best approach is to cancel all further testing such as the treadmill. We have scheduled a heart catherization for tomorrow morning at Redmond. We will send you by ambulance to Redmond. Your family will remain here. You will be returned to Floyd by ambulance when the procedure is complete and we have all the results. Any questions?" We said, "No." He explained someone would be in later to explain the procedure.

The doctor left after giving these instructions: "If you start hurting in your chest, call the nurse immediately. She will give you a nitroglycerin tablet to put under your tongue. If the pain doesn't stop in 20 minutes, call her again for another pill."

I wondered what in the world was happening to me. Am I falling apart at the young age of 49? I wasn't worried, but kept very quiet the remainder of the night. I was absolutely sure I was fine, but God's words kept ringing in my head, "BE STILL. YOU ARE HERE FOR YOUR

OWN GOOD." What is wrong that He should say that? If something is wrong, why doesn't God heal me? Faith was not an issue. There was a lot of prayer being offered for me and truthfully, I wasn't positive I was sick. If I wasn't sure I was sick, how could I believe for a healing that wasn't needed? Secondly, the Word states, *Faith cometh by hearing and hearing by the word of God* (Romans 10:17). Psalms 107:20(a) states, *He sent His Word, and healed them.* I definitely heard God speak to me, but He said absolutely nothing about healing me. He didn't even indicate I was healed. Without those healing words being spoken by Him, a miraculous healing was not in the plan of God for me.

The next morning the procedure was explained to Jane and me, telling us we really didn't have anything to worry about. It was a simple procedure and was done all the time. It was very common. They would put a tube in an artery in my leg at the groin and push the tube through the artery to my heart. They would then release some dye into my heart. They would watch on the video screen how the dye progressed through my heart and the related arteries and vessels. I would be able to watch on the monitor.

After about an hour, I was put into the ambulance and driven to Redmond Hospital for the procedure to be performed. I was taken to a room where doctors and nurses dressed in white were waiting. They were all very cordial and smiling. It looked as if a major surgical procedure was about to take place but they made me feel very comfortable. One of them walked over to me, asked how I was doing, and explained what they were about to do. He asked if I had any questions. I told him I didn't. He told me to watch the monitor and they would begin.

I could feel the injection that deadened the area in the groin where they were going to insert the tube. After that I felt nothing. I watched the monitor and could see the tube as it progressed up the artery to my chest area. I could see it as it curved with the artery and began the short descent toward my heart. I saw the dye released as it flowed through the arteries and through my heart. The tube was removed slowly and one of the attendants said, "It is over, you can relax now. The doctors are going to look at the video and will be with you in a moment."

I felt them put pressure on the tube entry point. The nurse said, "This will probably hurt a moment, but we will have to make sure it doesn't bleed." I said, "It's okay."

Suddenly my chest began to hurt intensely. The pressure, the pain in my chest and my neck was seemingly ten times greater than anything I had felt in previous days. I said, "Nurse, my chest is hurting." I heard her say, "Doctor," then I must have momentarily passed out. The next thing I heard was coming over the hospital speaker system, "Code Blue...Code Blue...Stat." I apparently lost consciousness again, because the next thing I knew the doctor was holding my chin, gently moving my head back and forth saying, "Mr. Tuten, Mr. Tuten wake up. That pain you are having is your heart. You have a 99% blockage in the main artery and we have to go in there immediately. You need to sign this consent. Mr. Tuten, can you hear me?" It was as if I could hear him but he was far away. I remember opening my eyes and in front of me through foggy vision I could see a clipboard and someone handing me a pen or pencil. They were saying, "Sign here, quick, sign here." I remember taking the pen with the help of the nurse and to the best of my ability, signing something. I could not see the paper or the place to sign. I just wrote something. Someone then said, "Good, get him prepped." That was all I remember. I don't know whether I was going in and out of consciousness or they were giving me some type of medication to heavily sedate me. Reality was nowhere to be found. I seemed to be in a state of half here and not here.

The next thing I knew, my name was being called again, and as I opened my eyes I saw my wife and children standing at my bed. They said they came in separately, but it seemed as if they were all there at one time. I was very groggy, but I remember saying, "I'm okay. Don't worry." I could see the anguish, concern and tears in their eyes. I wanted to say something else to them but I must have passed out again. The next time my eyes opened, I was being rapidly pushed down a hall on a gurney looking up at the lights as they passed overhead. We entered a room I remember to be very cold. I could see the nurses and doctors preparing for surgery. I remember seeing the big lights and the white, clean appearance of the room. At that moment I thought to myself, "They are going to cut me open and work on my heart. I only have one. What if something goes wrong?" Instantly, I felt the most beautiful peace come over me, as if to say "You are going to be fine." The nurse said, "We are going to give you something now to help you sleep." I could feel myself drifting off to sleep with the most beautiful peace imaginable. With that peace, I could have faced anything without doubt, fear, or trembling.

In what seemed to me like seconds, but was really 6½ hours later, I was being awakened in the recovery room by my doctor. As I opened my eyes he said, "Ed, this was a close call. If you had been anywhere but the hospital when this happened, you would not have made it." I drifted off to sleep again but remembered my mouth hurting. The nurse woke me up and I began pulling at the restraints on my arms because my mouth was hurting and I couldn't get to it. I couldn't tell her because I had all kinds of tubes in and on me including down my throat. I couldn't move and I couldn't speak. In a few minutes, Jane came into the room. She put her hand in mine. I began pulling her by the arm. She, thank God, had enough wisdom to understand I was trying to tell her something.

I would pull her arm and as she would give in to my pull, my hand would move further up her arm. I kept pulling and saying to myself, "Please Jane, don't stop." As I continued to pull, she kept getting closer and closer to the bed. Finally she got close enough, I pointed to her mouth and she said, "Your mouth, is something wrong with your mouth?" I shook my head, "Yes," and breathed a sigh of relief. She called the nurse over to my bed and told her something was wrong with my mouth. The nurse came to my bed and found when they put the breathing tube down my throat, they caught my bottom lip between my teeth and the tube. The tube, being a very tight fit and heavy, had my bottom lip pressed inward on the top of my bottom teeth and my teeth were literally slicing my lip. That pain was worse than any I was experiencing from the surgery. When she moved the tube and released my lip, I was fine. I had no pain. Not even from the surgery. I was cut from my knee to my ankle on my left leg so they could get an artery and was cut from my throat to the upper part of my stomach completely

154

through the breastbone. There were wires and tubes going everywhere with several entering my body at different places and absolutely no pain. I was truly amazed.

I was still very sleepy from the anesthesia. The nurse kept waking me for medications and to check vitals. I would go immediately back to sleep. During one of the visiting hours, I was awakened, and there stood my mother and brother. She had called several days earlier and asked Jane if she should come to Rome and Jane gave the phone to me. I told her it wasn't necessary because all I was having done was a heart cath. That, of course, was not the situation once the procedure was completed. They had driven from Savannah since I was far more critical than first thought. I was so glad to see them, but sorry it was under such difficult circumstances. I was in surgery during their trip, and they didn't know whether I was dead or alive until they got there late that night. I had lost all track of time. I wasn't sure whether it was day or night or even what time it was.

My prognosis was excellent and the remainder of my days in the hospital was fairly uneventful. I was moved out of recovery and intensive care to a regular room within a couple of days. I began the required walks up and down the hall to regain some strength. I was told when I walk the distance of the hall and back to my room twice, I could go home. I really pushed it. My recovery was remarkable even by the doctors' standards. I was quick to tell them a lot of people had been and still were praying for me. I believe my recovery was a true witness to the power of God, after all He did say I was there for my own good. I asked Jane and the children to go to church

Sunday morning and thank God for what He had done, while I thanked Him from my hospital bed.

I was released from the hospital on the seventh day after emergency three-bypass open-heart surgery. I now began a recovery period that ultimately resulted in me feeling like a new man. I felt better than I had felt in 15 years. I had more energy and more life about me. I wasn't dragging anymore to get up and go to work. I wasn't fighting fatigue on a constant basis. I was a new person. It was as if God had given me a second chance in life. I guess if the real truth were known, that is exactly what He did. Had I turned right that Tuesday morning in Rome to go home, I would have literally been home with the Lord in 48 hours. I would not have survived the trip to the hospital. With the condition I was in when the pain hit me so hard in the hospital immediately after the heart cath, I probably would not have been alive when the ambulance picked me up at home to take me to the hospital. God knew exactly what He was doing and why. I thank him to this day for that divine move in my life. It saved my life so I could finish His work He had called me to do.

I am convinced that satan had nothing to do with any of this. I believe he may have tried to get his rotten fingers in the situation but God was in total, complete control every second of every hour I was in danger. I believe this was a weakness of the body due to genetic predisposition. God proved Himself to be even more powerful than the blueprint laid down for our lives by our genes. After all He did create the genes and knows much more about them and their make-up than any scientist or physician collectively have ever known or will ever know.

The first Sunday evening I went back to church after going home was a powerful service. All I could do was thank God and praise Him for all He had done. My spirit was soaring, and I felt light as a feather. As I was standing at the altar continuing to thank and praise Him, I heard these words, "YOU WALKED THRU THE VALLEY OF THE SHADOW OF DEATH. YOU FEARED NO EVIL FOR I WAS WITH YOU. MY ROD AND MY STAFF COMFORTED YOU." That said it all. In a few divinely spoken words, my Lord summed up the entire scenario from the first day until now. He was there all the time.

Chapter 12
New Station....New Home

God had already spoken to broaden our borders
and we began to look at areas west of Cartersville. Areas
to the north, east, and south were virtually blocked in
regard to building new stations. It was possible to build
translators, which we did. New stations were completely
out of the question since by FCC rules and regulations
every frequency on the FM band was occupied by
stations either in or near Chattanooga, in or near Atlanta or
points between. We received the last available frequency
between these two cities when we were authorized
91.7 FM for WCCV. The only possibility was to buy an
existing station. This was completely prohibitive from
purely a cost factor. To buy an existing station in this area
between or in the two cities would start at multi-millions
of dollars. We had faith, but not quiet that much. God
was not specific in how to broaden our boarders, so we
looked at the area of least resistance. He did not speak to
buy anything, so I wasn't about to commit this ministry to
that much debt. Had He spoken to buy, I would have
without hesitation.

Since WCCV's signal was not reaching Rome or
Cedartown clearly, we decided to look in that direction.
Our consulting engineer did a frequency search and
determined Cedartown would be the better of the two
cities because of other stations and interference patterns.
Word got out we were considering the Cedartown area
for radio station number two. Mr. P. James (Papa)
Strickland, a landowner in the Cedartown area, offered a
mountain site to construct a tower free of land lease cost.

We filed an application with the FCC to build a tower on Mr. Strickland's property with the intention of simulcasting from WCCV through the Cedartown station to a new and larger listening audience. The new station would be stronger than WCCV and would cover a larger territory reaching into the Alabama area. The application was approved and we obtained the call letters WJCK, Where Jesus Christ is King.

WJCK signed on the air in April 1994, and the broadening of the boarders had begun. We received an excellent response from WJCK; however, our signal was not reaching into Rome, Georgia, clearly enough to enjoy. We had to protect a station in Chattanooga; consequently, our signal output toward the Rome area had to be reduced so we would not interfere with them.

The situation that occurred in the very beginning of the ministry, when I didn't have enough faith to file for a 3,000-watt station for Cartersville, was now coming back to torment me again as it would from time to time. "If only," I would say to myself, "I had made that one decision correctly we would not only be reaching Rome and Cedartown with an excellent signal from WCCV, but also Marietta, Acworth, Kennesaw, and other cities to the south and southeast of Cartersville." There are countless times I said to Jane and myself, "If only." Now there was nothing I could do to correct the error. With the translators and the second station that had been built, a large part of the area I feel was lost originally when I made that decision was recovered, but it wasn't the same. In different areas people had to change the radio dial to maintain a signal from WCCV, and I knew this was and is aggravating.

Several years passed and a gentleman, James Bennett from Piedmont, Alabama, contacted us about putting a station in his area. I contacted our consulting engineer and presented the request to him. He did his usual frequency search and found that we could move WJCK to Piedmont, greatly increasing the power at the same time. We considered this option. We discussed it as a staff, and I took it to the Board of Directors. They approved the move by stepping out on big faith because big money would be involved.

We filed the application with the FCC, and it was eventually approved after delays and governmental situations that were totally beyond our control. The adversary fought this move from the very beginning because he knew what a mighty force WJCK would be for the gospel of Jesus Christ. Every time we made an effort to accomplish something in regard to the move of WJCK, we were faced with conflict and indecision. Mr. Bennett, our contact in the Alabama area, was having the same problem. His business suffered, he suffered physically, and the staff at WCCV would have unpleasant, unexplainable situations occur in their personal lives. Problems would transpire at WCCV for which we had no explanation. We knew this wasn't God closing doors to stop the move and realized where the trouble originated. We began taking our rightful authority in the name of Jesus to fend off the evil that was trying to overtake and stop us.

When I know I am supposed to do something, especially something for God, and the adversary tries to stop me, I get more and more determined to do what God wants, and the fight is on. We know who the winner is going to be when the name of Jesus Christ is put in the face of the enemy. It isn't easy, but God never told me it would be easy. He told me it was going to be a lonely walk, but He and I would walk it together. My position is: If God is with me, who including the enemy, can and will be against me?

On March 7, 1999, WJCK Piedmont, Alabama, signed on the air after nearly four years of struggle, fight, and difficult decision-making. It has proven to be just what the enemy feared, a lighthouse shining in the darkness to lead and guide the way to our Lord Jesus Christ and His expectations of a Christian life. Response has been fantastic. The people of Northeast Alabama have participated in volunteer work, contributing their finances to keep it on the air, and they have prayed for WJCK and the staff. There are the usual complainers that can never be satisfied. I now believe they have been put here to knock off some edges that we as staff may be carrying around at times, as well as teaching us temperance and patience. We have resigned ourselves that those kind will always be with us, so we move ahead in God's plan and don't look back. The staff at WJCK worked tirelessly to make a successful radio station as did the staff at WCCV in the beginning. I believe each and every person involved, staff or volunteer, will reap a special reward for a job well done that furthered the kingdom of God by radio.

Even though WJCK had moved to Piedmont, that didn't help the signal coverage in Rome, and now Cedartown was without a decent signal because of the mountainous terrain between Piedmont and Cedartown. "What are we to do to correct this problem?" was my heart's cry to God. Hardly a day passed in which my thoughts weren't on the coverage problem of WCCV. WJCK was doing exactly what all of us had anticipated.

161

There wasn't a problem with coverage from that station, only WCCV.

In the meantime with the coverage situation constantly on my mind, the staff continued to grow, and space was rapidly being filled at our WCCV facilities on Main Street in Cartersville. The time finally approached that we had five people in one small office with desks butting up to each other. It was practically impossible to carry on a conversation on the phone because of the constant background noise emanating from the others in the room. A private conversation was totally impossible. I would occasionally remember the words God spoke to me many years ago, "PRAY FOR YOUR OWN FACILITIES." I would say to myself, "Wouldn't it be nice for each of us to have our own office where we could work without interference and noise?" I really held out no hope for this primarily because of our constant financial struggle. There was never any money left over at the end of the month, and more often than not there were more bills than money. This wasn't due to mismanagement of funds. The figures would prove it was primarily due to pledges of support not being kept.

Any ministry has not heard from God that doesn't struggle, especially in the beginning and during the maturing years, which can last 20 years or longer, to accomplish the goals established by God. I fully know as a ministry matures and grows, the struggle may not be as difficult as in the beginning, but there will still be a struggle. For example, a particular individual recently questioned the integrity of Immanuel Broadcasting because we always struggle so hard. The person making that statement obviously doesn't know about ministry and how God operates. That person wouldn't come to the station and pray with an intercessory prayer group that met here on a weekly basis to pray for the ministry. The person never came and asked for a financial statement or a percentage report of people who pledged support and never paid their pledge. The person never darkened the doors of my office to say, "Ed, I have some concerns about the ministry, may I talk to you?" We made it known the finances of this ministry were an open book. Any information desired was available to anyone upon request. The only information we would not release to anyone was the individual contributors and their contributions made to the ministry.

I was never told the name of this individual who made the statement, and I really don't want to know. I hold no malice or unforgiveness against that particular individual or anyone else that speaks in a derogatory manner about or against the ministry and the way it operates. I do pray for them when I think about it. I must say I am deeply hurt by these accusations as I am by any accusation that directly reflects on the ministry. It is the type of hurt that occurs when someone discredits or talks about your children in a critical and unforgiving manner. Everyone has a God-given and a constitutional right to their opinion, even though that opinion may be totally without fact. The point here is not to judge a ministry, a leader of a ministry, or one that is anointed of God, unless you have absolute proof of your judgmental accusations. If you suspect something or are just responding to rumor, go to the person or ministry in question and get the facts. God has a way of correcting error, disciplining people, and dealing with situations without the added input of individuals trying to rule from the outside to prove a point, which can and sometimes does destroy a ministry or persons in that ministry. In the meantime, God has a way of dealing with those that unjustly judge. The Bible plainly states: *Judge not, that you be not judged* (Matthew 7:1).

One day I wasn't really doing anything or even praying. I was just standing around thinking about things as I usually do. Suddenly, I saw myself standing in front of a large window from an upper floor looking out over a beautiful meadow with mountains in the background. The view was absolutely breathtaking. I was excited and shared with Jane and a few others what I had seen. I truthfully believed it to be the place of my retirement, the completion of my part of this multi-generational ministry and the closing days of my life that God was allowing me to see. He knew I loved the mountains and beautiful scenery. I believed God was giving me a glimpse of the future and allowing me to see what I had to look forward to. However, the passing of time proved what I believed the vision to be and what God actually meant it to be were two different things.

On the birthday of my grandson, Drew Barnette, July 12, 1992, Jane and I were at my daughter's and son-in-law's home with all the family talking and sharing as families do at family gatherings. Without warning the voice of God rumbled in my spirit these words, "YOU HAVE 20 YEARS TO FINISH DOING WHAT I HAVE CALLED YOU TO DO." Startled to the bone, I began doing some quick math and realized He was saying I have until the year 2012 to finish what He has told me to do. I figured since He spoke to me in July, He meant July of 2012. I was stunned. Today, I can still hear those words ringing in my spirit with the same authority and love in which they were spoken.

164

I was sitting at home one evening and saw an ad in the newspaper concerning computer classes with classes starting at the foundation of the modern computer systems. Since the ministry was becoming very computer oriented and the technology was nothing like it was when I was in computer operations years ago, I thought it would be a good idea for me to take some courses, so I would at least know what these men and women were talking about. I called the school the next day and registered for the first class.

When the day finally arrived, I called the school to confirm my enrollment and to make sure I had the correct address. I thought to myself, "That is just around the corner so I can leave about ten minutes before class starts and get there on time." Little did I know God was about to reveal another miracle and make a mighty move in this ministry. I left the office and began my journey to school. I hadn't been to school in years and was looking forward to it. I turned on Erwin Street headed for what I thought was the school. I kept driving and looking but couldn't find the address. I got almost to the end of Erwin Street. The Lewis Carpet Mill administration building which I helped design in the distant past was in this vicinity. I had driven there many times going to work. I planned to turn around in the parking lot and go the other way on Erwin Street, thinking I had misunderstood the directions and should have gone north rather than south. Maybe the school was on North Erwin and not South Erwin. I truthfully don't remember them giving me a direction with the address. I guess I assumed South Erwin. I now know that it wasn't an assumption but the guiding hand of God directing me to a place that would fulfill a word from Him 15 years prior. It was the next step for Immanuel

Broadcasting to take in preparation for the future yet to be revealed.

I began to slow down so I could turn around, and the building came into view. I remembered the construction phase and all the days and nights of hard work that transpired during the time the carpet mill occupied the building. It was now vacant, and I have to admit it did look rather lonely standing there shining in the bright sun. I remembered the day I left the mill for the last time and how I never wanted to see this building again. I had literally learned to grossly dislike the place. I would purposely avoid this end of Erwin Street so I wouldn't have to pass by here. There is absolutely nothing wrong with carpet mill employment. It is an honorable and very valuable profession in today's world economics. The truth was God had to make me hate my job so I would quit before He started working on me, because I did love it dearly. He knew I wouldn't quit as long as I was happy and satisfied with my work. As I reached the parking area I saw the post that was built originally to put the Lewis Carpet Mill sign and address on. On that post now was not Lewis Carpet Mill but a for sale sign. The only way I can describe what happened was it felt like a knife had been driven into my gut. I didn't hear a word. The Lord didn't speak but I knew…that I knew…that I knew this was to be the new home of Immanuel Broadcasting Network. "I can't believe this," were my words speaking loudly to myself.

Suddenly, I saw the building in a totally different perspective. The Lord immediately altered my entire thinking process. God had this building built many years ago waiting for Immanuel Broadcasting Network to come forth from the dust of the earth and grow to a point of maturity that it would need this building to operate as He intended. He had used me to help with the original design, and I wasn't even a Christian at the time. There was a long way to go in procuring the facilities, but I knew God had worked another miracle, and He was going to see this project through to its completion.

I wrote down the name of the realtor and returned to the office. School was now taking a back seat. I called the realtor about the building and asked if I could look at it. He agreed and we made arrangements to meet. Upon arriving at the site, he unlocked the door, and we proceeded to go inside. Memories began flooding my mind as I walked through the building. From room to room I could see the activity that once transpired even though they were now bare, empty, and cold. There had been a great deal of water damage where the pipes had burst in the walls because the previous tenant did not drain the lines when they left. I could see a lot of work that needed to be done and a lot of money needed to do that work. As we proceeded through the building we went upstairs where the accounting and administrative offices were once located. It too was empty, but in my memory I could still hear the adding machines clicking and the typewriters pounding as the business of the carpet mill was processed daily. Those memories were now pleasant. Greg, the realtor, and I walked into the office that was once the chief administrator's office where the balcony had been built many years earlier to set his office apart from all the others. I walked to the vertical blinds that were closed and asked Greg if I could open them. He said I could. I pulled the cord and the blinds began to open slowly. When they were completely opened I was suddenly thrust into the vision I had seen several months earlier. There was the upper floor, the large window, the meadow and the mountains in the background just as I had seen a few months earlier and thought it was my retirement vision. Instead, God was showing me the new home of Immanuel Broadcasting Network. I immediately had confirmation in my spirit that our own facilities had been found.

I told Greg I was definitely interested and we needed to talk more. He said he had time to talk now. We talked about the current owners, the condition of the building, and of course the price. He said the owners were asking $275,000, which was considerably less than a year ago because of all the water damage. The building was to be purchased as is. Having seen the original construction, I knew the building was solid and would be here for a long time to come. It was all concrete and steel and virtually fireproof.

I told him I thought the price was fair and asked, "What do I do now?" He said the next thing would be for me to make a counteroffer. I knew nothing about real estate and had no idea how to determine a counteroffer. I was once again thrust into a situation I knew nothing about, but by now I was getting accustomed to it. I knew whom to ask for answers. This was on Friday. On Sunday morning I asked the members of the small church I had in my home to lay hands on me and ask God to give me wisdom in this matter. I needed to know what counteroffer to make the owners. As they began to stand and walk toward me, God spoke to me "$250,000." I immediately told them I had my answer.

The next morning I called Greg and told him my counteroffer was $250,000. He said, "Ed, I don't know if they will accept that or not. It is awfully low in comparison to what they asked." I told him that was my one and only offer. I explained that God had given me that amount. That was my counteroffer. He said, "Alright, I will call them." About an hour later he called me back and said, "Ed, they have accepted your offer. I am really surprised." I didn't tell him but I wasn't surprised. God said it, I believed it, and that settled it.

I called the Board of Directors together at the building to explain the entire situation. At this point I needed their decision to proceed or stop. As they began to arrive, some of them literally broke into tears and said, "Ed, I feel God in this place." When all were present I explained the entire story to them. All of us toured the building. I told them, in my mind, how all of this would be accomplished. Comments came forth such as, "This is of God," "God has surely ordained this move," and "This is where God wants us." We discussed the pros and cons, the financing, and all of the ramifications of a move of this nature. It was now time to vote. I presented the motion that the building at 779 South Erwin Street be purchased and renovated for the home of Immanuel Broadcasting Network. The motion was seconded. I presented the opportunity to vote and all immediately voted in the affirmative. It was unanimous, not one descent. The stage was set, and we began to move forward.

At this time Immanuel Broadcasting Network was operating totally debt free and had been for several years. It felt good. I really didn't want to borrow money, because I knew the building purchase was only the beginning. There was new equipment to purchase because we didn't want to go off the air for two or three weeks while the equipment in the old building was being disassembled and installed in the new. There was furnishings to buy since the new building had three times the floor space as the old one. All I could see was money, money, money. I prayed for God to supply this money. We certainly didn't have these kinds of reserves, and I certainly didn't have it personally. One morning I was sitting at my desk rather forlorn and Howard, my son, came in for his workday. Knowing me well, he asked me what was wrong. I expressed to him I did not want to borrow money for this move, but I knew the move was straight from the hands of God, and I didn't know what to do. He said to me, "What does the Bible say about the wealth of the wicked?" I replied, *The wealth of the sinner* (wicked) *is laid* (stored) *up for the just* (righteous) (Proverbs 14:22b). He said, "Where is it stored?" I thought a moment and said, "In the banks." "That is correct," he said. "Now go to the bank and get the money that has been put there so Immanuel Broadcasting Network can have its new home." It was as if a light of revelation came on and the hesitancy was gone. The process of borrowing the money began.

Getting the money together, constructing the inside to accommodate a radio station, arguing with contractors, and the general headaches of a building project, all contributed to a year and a half of work getting the building ready for Immanuel Broadcasting Network to occupy. Finally, in September 1998, we moved into an unfinished building. In January 1999, we held a service dedicating the building and its purpose to the Almighty God who had already spoken, "MY GLORY IS ON THAT PLACE." It was now our job to let the people see His glory as the gospel of Jesus Christ began emanating from 779 South Erwin Street, Cartersville, Georgia, going around the world via the World Wide Web. Fifteen years after God said, "PRAY FOR YOUR OWN FACILITIES," we were occupying a true gift from God, our own beautiful home.

Chapter 13
Near Financial Demise

In the beginning after God spoke to us to, "ASK AND WE WOULD RECEIVE," we have unashamedly conducted fundraising events usually twice annually to raise the operating and growth budget for the next six months. People have objected, have turned the station off, and have criticized us for raising money on the air. We have been accused of begging and trying to manipulate people with a various array of tongue lashings in an attempt to make us conform to the world's way of functioning, completely ignoring the Kingdom Principle of allowing people the right and privilege to give to God so they can receive. It is not generally realized there are numerous people who proclaim Christ as Lord but never darken the doors of a church. They don't like organized religion or they have been hurt terribly by a Christian in a church or by the church itself. In a large number of instances, people are unable to get to church on a given worship day. These are voids. These are situations where the body of Christ needs to come to the aid of the less fortunate whether that is financially, emotionally, or spiritually.

This is where radio plays a major role in filling the void. It is a very efficient way of spreading the Gospel to the lost and bringing church to homes when no one else can or will. Television is a great, colorful medium for the gospel to be presented, but it has its shortcomings. There are a number of people that either don't have TV, or if they do, they can't afford the cable or satellite rates that seemingly continue to rise with never-ending ceilings. This prohibits them from receiving most of the Christian programming, because they are brought in by cable and not the airways, as with radio. The cost of radio in your home is very cheap and the most powerful medium available to spread the gospel to the unchurched and the lost. Radio will reach into places that television will never go purely because of the nature and cost of the medium.

This is why I believe God wants His people to support Christian radio as they do television. The people who can't afford it, need it. The people who need it, don't have it. God's people can make a difference.

Immanuel Broadcasting is part of what God has placed here to reach His people. Church gatherings occur two or three days a week for a few total hours each week. Christian radio is here twenty-four hours a day, seven days a week to feed the body of Christ where they live, in the home, car, or business. So that is why we have Share Time.

A gentleman once said to me, "Ed, if you were given one million dollars today, you would probably still try and raise money." I didn't answer him at the time but the truth of the matter is, I would do exactly that. I will always give the listeners an opportunity to give to God's work so they can be blessed. The results of giving to God's work, in this instance, Immanuel Broadcasting, is not only the giver being blessed but the ministry of God continuing to progressively move forward in God's Kingdom.

There has never, never been a purpose to "fatten" the pocketbooks of the ministry or anyone involved. There are no perks such as allowances for automobiles, houses, or expenses, and the payroll is absolutely in line with the non-commercial radio broadcasting industry according to surveys we obtain to keep us informed. We as staff and management of Immanuel Broadcasting have never asked for a dime that was not needed to operate or use in a special project. We have never spent monies unnecessarily in the operation and maintenance of this ministry.

Our Share Time budgets are figured very tightly in an effort to avoid asking for more than needed. This is why there is a shortage of money at certain times of the year. The budget is figured for that particular season, but people, for various reasons, do not keep their commitments made during the Share Time event.

Share Time is also a time for more concentrated ministry. All programming schedules are cancelled, relieving the timing element of talk, music, and programming. There is much more freedom and consequently a keener sensitivity to God's Spirit and what He desires.

In October 1997, we conducted our Fall Share '97 Share Time, taking pledges for a 12-month period, rather than six months as usual. The hope was we would be able to reduce the number of Share Times each year. We also knew we were scheduled, at that time, to move into the new building sometime during the spring or early summer of 1998. If this move occurred as scheduled, we would not be able to conduct our Spring Share '98, as we would usually do.

Fall Share '97 began by asking for 12-month pledges. As the Share Time progressed we could readily see it appeared this was going to work. People called in making monthly pledges or commitments for a year and we were very close to reaching the goal when Share Time was over.

We felt all was fine and trusted the fact that enough money was pledged to pay all the bills through the end of September 1998. As the days progressed, moving day in the spring did not materialize; neither did moving day in early summer. Something else was also failing to materialize. The pledges made in Fall Share '97 were not coming in as promised. It was obvious, if this trend continued we were going to be in bad trouble by summer's end. We had to begin drawing from our reserve account to pay our bills and pay the payroll. Soon that reserve was exhausted. The bills we were unable to pay began mounting up.

Here we were near the end of the construction phase, our money gone and no place to get any. Creditors were calling wanting their money. We didn't have any to give them. It became very embarrassing to tell these people we were broke. We made pleas on the air and there was some relief, but not near enough.

The tearing down phase from the old building and putting into the new had begun. Part of us was one place and the remainder at another. Time was moving on and the bills continued to pile on top of each other. On September 21, 1998, we completed the move to our new home. In that move we carried unpaid bills for June, July, August, and September. Our reserve was gone and no one was getting paid, not even the power company. A few days after we had moved, I was in my office trying to put away files and set up my desk. I heard a thundering noise. Shannon, our bookkeeper was running up the stairs in a panic. She burst into my office and said, "Ed, the power company is here to turn off the power because we have not paid them." I asked, "How much do we owe them?" "A little over one thousand dollars," was the answer. I asked, "How much do we have in the bank?" "Not enough," was the reply. I tried not to show it, but I was also panicking. I asked how much was in the reserve (savings) account and how much came in the mail. Shannon did some quick math and informed me that with all that was left and what came in the mail, we had enough to write a check for the power bill with a very few dollars remaining. I said, "Write the check. We have to keep the power on if nothing else is paid."

Thank God, His provision was sufficient. I was also thanking God this was Friday and Fall Share '98 would begin Monday. Maybe we could get some relief from the financial debacle we were in. At the close of the day on Friday we were sitting on $180,000 in unpaid bills. I was nearly a basket case, but I knew I had to trust God to see us through.

Fall Share '98 began. We went on the air advising people of the seriousness of our situation and how close we came to completely being off the air due to no power. People responded tremendously and all seemed to be off to a good start. Funds were coming in and we had begun to catch up on some of the backlog. It was a slow process but at least progress was being made and our creditors were getting happier and happier.

As Share Time ended, God in His sovereignty, sent enough money to pay the bills until they were current. What a feeling. Everything paid. No one was hounding us for money. It was a nice feeling and a tremendous relief. It was almost like a new day here at the ministry. We were now in our new building. All bills were current and the money was coming in to keep them current, at least for a while. I did not know another deeper valley was immediately around the corner.

When we needed to borrow money to purchase and remodel the building that would eventually become the home of Immanuel Broadcasting, I went to a couple of banks in Cartersville. I had dealt with these banks in the past and knew some of the loan officers, as well as other employees personally. I had dealt with one particular bank for many years. I felt very comfortable talking to them about a loan for the building and the construction. They knew me and knew about WCCV. All of them eventually turned me down due to lack of collateral and the fact we were a non-commercial radio station. I wasn't angry but didn't know where to turn for the money.

Through a service that helps radio and TV stations find people or organizations that will fund various projects, a bank was located in Cartersville that agreed to look at the project and talk to me. I had never dealt with this bank and didn't know anyone working there. For the purpose of the book I will call this bank Shellman's Bank. The service that located the bank made an appointment for me to meet with them. When I arrived at the bank I was introduced to Brian Edwards, the loan officer. I explained to him the need for the loan and what we were trying to accomplish.

Brian informed me he remembered when the station signed on many years ago. He was a little boy riding with his mother in their car on that day in January 1983. She had the radio tuned to 91.7 waiting for us to sign on. When the music began for the very first time, he said she shouted. He had never heard his mother do that before.

We talked a few minutes. He gave me a list of paperwork he would need to process the loan and take it before the committee. I gathered all he requested, took it to him, and waited. A few days later, Brian called me and informed me the loan had been approved. Needless to say, I was ecstatic. That is when work began on the new building.

Brian and I both had discussed the need for money later to buy the new equipment and some furnishings for the new facility. The equipment was necessary for two reasons. One was to move forward with more up-to-date broadcast technology. Second and more importantly, we would need to install and test the new equipment in the new building before moving out of the old building. If we didn't, WCCV would be off the air for several weeks while the equipment was disconnected, moved, installed, and tested in the new building. I wasn't willing to do that. Brian stated when we got to that point, call him and we would look at it.

The time came in early 1998 when the equipment was needed. Brian and I worked out a loan that I felt we could pay back in six months because I knew Fall Share '98 would be held before the due date. I signed a note to pay the loan back at the end of October in full, only paying interest until that time. Fall Share came and went. It didn't happen. There was enough money raised to meet our monthly obligations, including the building mortgage, but not the equipment loan. What was I going to do? I knew the loan was due in full and I knew the grace period was running out.

I went to Shellman's Bank to talk to Brian about it, but he had left the bank. Now I was talking to a stranger who knew nothing about us or about the ministry. I explained to him what happened. He wanted to know when I would be able to get the money. I told him I didn't know how, when, or where I would get it. I really didn't know what to do about it. I knew I owed it but my hands were tied. The amount was approximately $80,000 and that was completely out of my personal league.

At several meetings I tried to get them to cash in a $50,000 CD they were holding as collateral, refinancing the note using the CD, and letting us make payments. They refused, stating the CD was their collateral and cashing it in, applying it to the outstanding loan, would be dissolving the only collateral they had. I am not a banker and know very little about banking procedures and policies, but that seemed a little ridiculous to me. However, I couldn't force the issue, especially from the position I was in. I went to my office really worried about what I could do and what was going to happen.

One day I received a bundle of paperwork to be filled out from Shellman's Bank. The questions indicated to me a take over of the operation and management of Immanuel Broadcasting was immanent. It appeared they were going to put a lock-box on our mail and handle all contributions through their system, taking it completely out of our hands. I called the bank and my interpretation of the documents was correct; however, that action was not being taken at that time. They just wanted the information in the event the action was forthcoming. I was sure that would be the end result, because I had no way of paying the money, and they wouldn't refinance. They had the right to take those steps because IBN had defaulted on the note. Defaulting on one note caused the mortgage, which was current, to go into default. That was the way the papers were drawn originally. I was sick. I refused to answer any questions on those forms and had absolutely no intention of sending them back to Shellman's Bank. I knew I had stepped out on God's bidding for this building and nobody or no bank was going to take this ministry out of our hands. I threw the papers in the trash and cried out to God for help. This was His ministry, and I was as confident as the day He spoke to me to build the station, He was somehow going to take care of this. How, was beyond my wildest imagination.

I never contacted Shellman's Bank again for any reason. I knew something would have to happen quickly, or I would really be on the hot seat. The next morning I was walking down the stairs at the station, and I heard, "BRIAN EDWARDS." Where is Brian, I thought? I knew he left Shellman's Bank but I wasn't sure where he went. I asked around the station and someone said, "He is at the new SunTrust Bank that is about to open." I called and asked for Brian. He immediately came to the phone. I shared what happened with Shellman's Bank. He asked if I could come to his office. He requested I bring certain papers with me. For some strange but believable reason I felt relief in my spirit like everything was going to be all right.

I took the papers to Brian. He sat there a few minutes while looking over them, asked a few questions and said, "Ed, I believe we can handle this. We will be able to refinance the original mortgage on the building purchase, cash in the CD paying off the debt incurred when moving WJCK from Cedartown, Georgia to Piedmont, Alabama, and combine the remainder into one note for five years. SunTrust will pay off Shellman's and you won't have to deal with the situation. I will take care of getting the final balances and paying them. I will call you when we are ready to sign the loans.

I left Brian's office in tears. How could one bank be so lenient and helpful while another is so dogmatic and legalistic? I thought rules were rules. It was behind me now and God had won another in a long series of victories keeping Immanuel Broadcasting in His sovereign hands. God through the willingness and understanding of Brian Edwards and SunTrust Bank had saved Immanuel Broadcasting. Thank God for people and institutions such as Brian Edwards and SunTrust Bank who will go the extra mile when the going gets tough, holding out a caring, helping hand without condemnation.

Chapter 14
Restitution...Almost

I have a large, framed wall map in my office that shows the two radio stations and all the translators. On this map is drawn the lines of the anticipated coverage area of each station or translator. It is very easy to see that WCCV doesn't put a good signal into Rome, Cedartown, Calhoun, Acworth, Kennesaw, and the list goes on. As I stated earlier, each time I look at this map I remember the day I lacked faith to believe God could supply the need for a larger station as much as He could the smaller. I distinctly remember discarding in my thoughts the 3,000-watt station for the 100-watt station that later became 910 watts. Over the years, I have regretted with agony that one decision made in the consulting engineer's office that fateful day in 1979 more than any other decision made over the span of time from then until now.

God has been merciful in providing places and finances to build the translators in various cities; however, this did not rectify my mistake. People were still not able to receive WCCV at 91.7 FM in the surrounding cities as I had hoped. I had a difficult time forgiving myself, but I knew God had forgiven me. I had asked for His forgiveness and continued on with the ministry, but forgiving myself was another story. I didn't let that stop me from moving forward and allowing the ministry to grow and prosper, but occasionally my thoughts would return to that day.

I practically have the map memorized, because over the years I have looked at it over and over and over. One day I was driving on Tennessee Street, a main thoroughfare in Cartersville. Quite suddenly I could see on my windshield that map in my office. I really thought I was losing it. The stress at the ministry, working a full-time job at the post office, and leading a small church in my home was really taking its toll on me. There appeared on the map I was seeing, a blinking red dot situated between Cartersville and Rome near the Floyd County line. Then the map disappeared as quickly as it appeared. It only lasted but a brief moment; however, I knew what I had seen and I knew what God was telling me. It was as if this information was placed in my spirit without a literal word being spoken. God was telling me that if I moved our transmitting facilities from Ponders Mountain where it had been all this time, to a place on the other side of the county going west, I could increase the power of the radio station. This was the thing for which I had been praying. I immediately thought, God was about to let me rectify my error.

I rushed to the station and checked the map at the exact spot I saw the blinking red light and there was a mountain named Mullinax. I called Kirk, our consulting engineer to tell him what happened and that I wanted to check into moving our transmitting facilities to that site. He said, "Ed, that won't do you any good. You still have to protect the stations in Atlanta, Cumming, and Chattanooga." I said, "Kirk, we are protecting those stations now and we are looking at moving a number of miles away from those areas." He said, "I will check it out and call you back."

I left the station and went to White, Georgia, where Howard had a small hair salon. I usually went there for him to cut my hair. After the 15 or 20-mile trip I arrived there on time for my appointment. When I walked in the door he said, "Dad, call Kirk, he needs to speak to you." I immediately returned his call and he said, "Ed, I have checked this thing out, and you can move to the Mullinax Mountain site and increase your power from 910 watts to 10,000 watts with a directional antenna." I was ecstatic. I could hardly believe my ears. I replied to him, "Let's do it. I will send you the statistics you need in the morning."

On February 26, 1997, I filed an application with the FCC to accomplish what I firmly believe God had shown me at the same time believing it was restitution time. He was going to allow me, at least in part, to compensate for my terrible mistake in the beginning. The waiting process now began. After a few months passed our application was returned because of an error made. The engineer corrected the error and in October 1997, the corrected application was filed with the Federal Communications Commission. Now another waiting game was in progress.

After the FCC checks and processes an application and finds it is clean and acceptable, they issue what is termed a "cut-off" list. This is a listing of all radio and television stations they have processed since the last list was prepared. On this list is information concerning the proposed facility such as city, power, type of station, and frequency. The purpose of this list is to advise the general public, as well as other stations, of the pending station to be built and its location. On the list is a date after which no one can file an opposing application or a complaint about any of the ones mentioned on the listing. Our cut-off date, the last date anyone could file against us for another station or a complaint about our application, was June 19, 1998, at midnight. On June 20, I went to the station and felt that we had cleared that last hurdle and now we would be getting a construction permit in a few weeks. We could start the long arduous process of moving our facilities from Ponders Mountain to Mullinax Mountain. Moving a transmitter site isn't as simple as driving a pick-up truck to the site, loading a few items, hauling it to the new site, setting it up, and turning it on. There is a huge tower, in this case 650 feet, to be purchased and built, an antenna pattern to farm out to the antenna companies to build and test, not to mention the ongoing process of site preparation, ground to be leveled, paths cut to guy wire anchor sites, power and phone lines installed, and the list goes on. Of course a secure, weatherproof building has to be constructed to house all of the expensive equipment. It is very similar to constructing a domestic house from the ground up but on a smaller scale. All of the same elements are there.

On July 22, 1998, I received an envelope with a return address of the Federal Communications Commission. Excitedly I told the staff, "Here is what we have been waiting for, the construction permit for the new WCCV."

I opened the letter and much to my dismay it wasn't the construction permit as expected. It was a letter from the FCC stating that another organization had filed an application that was received by the Commission just a few hours before the deadline. The application was for a station to be built on frequency 91.7 FM in a small city in east- central Alabama that was going to cause interference with both stations since they were each on the same frequency. The cities were too close together, and it violated FCC rules and regulations to authorize both. I checked out the organization and found I knew the individual that was in charge of the other organization. I immediately wrote him a letter and tried to explain the situation to him, stating we only had a couple of months to clear up the problem or the FCC would reject both applications and we would have to start over. It had already been 17 months since our first application was filed, and I didn't want to waste any more time in constructing the new WCCV.

In a few days he called and set up an appointment for us to meet at the WCCV studios. He arrived on the day scheduled, and we talked about the ministry in a rather congenial manner. I showed him the map on my wall and explained everything I could to him about our efforts, our plans, and what we had on the drawing board. I took him to the building we had just purchased for our new home. He politely listened, and when I was finished we went to lunch.

Upon returning from lunch he stated that he had a proposal for me. I said we could discuss it. I felt I could trust him since I had known him for several years. I was totally astonished at his reply. His proposal basically stated that I give him the WCCV broadcasting license, the new building, the Marietta translator, and the Woodstock translator. He would in turn supply finances, give me a construction permit he had for a station in LaGrange, Georgia, and one he had in Jasper, Georgia, and I could have all of the Alabama facility. I was stunned that anyone would even have the nerve to make such a proposal. I said, "In other words you want me to give you everything I have worked for the last 14 years and basically start over with stations that aren't even on the air." He replied, "You could move to LaGrange or to Alabama and have the same thing you have here. You wouldn't have the financial struggles you have now and you would have basically the same setup you have at the present." I couldn't believe my ears, but yet I heard everything he said. He went on to say that he wanted to get into the Atlanta area with FM radio, and WCCV with the Marietta and Woodstock translators would be his ticket since there were not any remaining frequencies in the area to build another station.

After he left I was quite shaken. I had tried to explain to him how God had directed me to build this station and to release it to anyone would put me in direct disobedience to Him. I wasn't willing to do that. I knew in my spirit his proposal was not of God, but I also felt I had to pursue every avenue of authority available to me. I had a Board of Directors meeting and needless to say the proposal didn't get off the table before there was a resounding and unanimous, "NO."

The individual would not even accept their decision. He kept telling me his deal was a win/win situation. All I could see was him winning and Immanuel Broadcasting losing. This was not a win/win deal. It was a lose/lose situation, and I was not about to partake of such an ungodly proposal. I guess he figured the dollars would be a magnet to draw me into his plan, but money is not the most important thing in the world to this ministry or me. It certainly isn't a decoy to draw me away from the calling of God on my life and His direction in that calling.

I tried everything to persuade him to cancel or change his competing application but to no avail. I had our consulting engineer look for another frequency in that town. He did and one was available. I asked him to prepare an application to change the frequency of the opposing application from 91.7 to the new frequency. I wrote a letter explaining the situation and sent a copy of that letter to the individual and his wife who had signed the original application. All she had to do was sign the application, return it to me in an envelope I had enclosed, and I would send it to the FCC at no cost to them. Both our problems would be cleared with the pending applications and they would approve both of them and construction could begin. He refused. He was still after his initial win/win proposal, but I could not and would not ever agree to a proposal such as that. He was literally using his competing application as a weapon to persuade me to agree to his plan. It was as if he was saying take my offer or WCCV will suffer in its power increase.

I finally called our engineer and asked what it would do if we filed an amendment to our application preparing it to protect the application he had filed against us. After a day or two the engineer called me back and said, "Ed, if you reduce your power from 10,000 watts to 7,300 watts your application will be acceptable because it will no longer interfere with his. I said, "Go ahead because he isn't going to budge and I am certainly not willing to throw this power increase away, because I know God showed it to me." He filed an amendment to our original application and the FCC began work on it.

I knew this process would take a while. I was eventually able to shake off all of this turmoil and proceed with the building project. We still had to do a great deal of work in the new building before we could occupy it. During the construction process when I would think about the application and having to reduce our power because of this situation, it would truly irritate me. I would pray and ask God to touch this man's heart and change his mind about the situation so he would cancel his application. I would ask the Lord to touch me and help me correct my attitude about the entire thing. God says vengeance is His. I prayed then and continue to pray that

He won't take His vengeance out on those that hinder the vision He has put forth for this ministry as has happened in this particular situation.

I could readily see that a reduction of 2,700 watts was going to reduce our potential listening area and this continued to trouble me. I called Kirk, our consulting engineer, and talked to him about it. He confirmed that we would possibly lose about 200,000 potential listeners. He said, "Ed, why don't you contact him and ask him to sell you his construction permit?" By now both applications had been approved and construction permits issued. I wrote him one more time asking if I could buy his permit, which was perfectly legal. I thought if I could purchase it, I would file a cancellation of his permit and file another amendment to ours, raising our power back to 10,000 watts and all would be back where it should be.

For someone to build a non-commercial station with limited available power, 400 watts, and the antenna at ground level, I felt would be to no avail. The coverage of an FM radio station is almost as dependent on height of the antenna above the ground as it is power output to obtain adequate coverage. Our radio station in Alabama, WJCK, covered this same area like a blanket with the gospel of Jesus Christ. The service to that area in east-central Alabama would be virtually duplicated. He, of course, has the right to build anywhere the FCC allows, and I don't fault him for that, but an area that small would have a difficult time supporting two full-time, non-commercial Christian stations.

In a few days I received his response to my offer to purchase his construction permit. He replied that he wasn't interested in the money, all he wanted was the

Atlanta area to bring quality programming with professional announcers to the listening audience. He went on to state that his offer was still open and he continued to feel his offer was a win/win situation for both of us, and the permit wasn't for sale. I wasn't going to address that issue again so I didn't answer his letter, since there wasn't really an answer to give. I could have been ugly but to what purpose. He had his belief about the way things should be and I had God's Word. He obviously didn't think WCCV was good enough to reach into the Atlanta area. The two operational ideologies were diabolically opposed to each other, and I could see neither was going to budge. That was my last try, and we continued with the reduced power permit we were issued, not realizing that it was going to cause more problems in the near future.

When a station has to protect adjacent towns and cities with radio stations that are close on the dial, an antenna has to be designed that will send just enough signal in each direction to gain the full capability of your station, yet not interfere with the ones next to you or even the second one away from you on the FM dial. This type of antenna is called a Directional Antenna. It gets it name from the fact that the signal it produces is directional in its pattern and the way the signal is broadcast. These antennas have to be specifically designed, built, and tested according to FCC specifications. Those specifications are very strict and leave very little room for error. Once the antenna is designed on paper, it has to be approved before it is constructed. Needless to say, these antennas are very expensive and time consuming to build and install.

I farmed the antenna pattern out to several antenna companies for pricing, trying to get the lowest price with the best quality. Each company came back and stated they couldn't build it because of the tightness of the pattern. I didn't understand this, so I called Kirk and asked him what the trouble was. He said, "Ed, because of the application that was filed against us we had to pull that side of the pattern so tight to prevent interference that it's making it very difficult for the antenna companies to comply with the requirements. It is, however, possible to build. It is just going to take some extra sharp engineering on the part of the antenna manufacturers."

All of the companies but one refused to consider it because of the difficulty factor. I received a proposal from them stating they could construct the antenna, and they gave me the cost. I signed the contract, sent them their required down payment, and began waiting, again. Several weeks later I received a phone call stating they had constructed a mock-up of the antenna using the correct parameters, but they could not make it work. They would have to go to a different antenna type and design, which was more expensive to build, but would not charge me extra since they had already quoted me.

Finally, all of the pieces started coming together to increase WCCV's power to 7,300 watts. All of the construction and approvals were finally complete. On March 28, 2001, WCCV changed from 910 watts to 7,300 watts of power. Immediately a reception problem was noticed in the area east and southeast of the tower, including the Cartersville area. At this same time we received a letter in the mail from a station in Cleveland, Tennessee. They had increased their power and because of their increase we would have to shut down our translator in Rossville, Georgia. This was a blow. I remember telling Neil Hopper, my right-hand man, that I sure was glad it wasn't our Woodstock or Marietta translator. One week later I received a letter in the mail that a station had gone on the air in Atlanta after many years of litigation in the courts. The station was one step up on the dial from our Woodstock translator. This meant the translator was interfering with their station, so the translator would have to be shut down. The Marietta translator was receiving its signal to broadcast from the Woodstock translator. When we shut down the Woodstock translator, it automatically shut down the Marietta translator. Here we were, in three week's time, losing three translators and increasing power to the parent station in which a bad signal was being broadcast in at least one direction, towards Cartersville, the city of license. Translators are considered a secondary service, and if a regular station comes into the area of a translator and interference is created, the translator has to go off the air no matter how long it has been there or the fact it came first.

Our spring Share Time was to begin April 1 and here we were with three translators short, a bad signal, and all bills still needing to be paid. It made for a less than successful fundraising event, but God is sufficient to supply all our need according to his riches in glory by Christ Jesus.

It is my prayer that the gentleman, who filed against us in the beginning, will realize what he has done and make restitution by canceling his conflicting permit and allow us to go to 10,000 watts as originally planned. I will never bow to the plan of giving up this ministry to him or anyone else unless God Almighty Himself gives me a direct Word from and through His Spirit. It will have to be spoken to me and not through someone else.

Since our power increase, we have been able to purchase the necessary equipment and put the Marietta translator back on the air. It now receives a signal from the parent station WCCV in Cartersville, which was impossible before the increase. I thank God for His providence and protection over the years to Immanuel Broadcasting and for the leading and guidance He has given the Board of Directors, the staff, and me.

What He told me in the beginning, "IT WILL BE A LONELY WALK SON, BUT YOU AND I WILL WALK IT TOGETHER," has been a reality. Now there are people that share the complete vision and are striving to fulfill that vision as God leads us down that path to completion.

Chapter 15
In Summary

When God calls an individual to do something, He imparts the gifts necessary to get that project at least started, and more often than not, the impartation is sufficient to complete the task. The scripture is very clear the gifts and calling of God are without repentance. This means in order to be obedient to the Word of the Lord revealed to you, there is no choice but to do it. Not to do it is disobedience, and disobedience is sin. The way you repent from sin is to do a 180-degree turn from what you are doing. In other words, go or do the opposite from your present direction or circumstances. To turn from the disobedience of not following God's calling is to do as He has asked.

So many times we as humans see things through eyes that best accommodate our place in life at the time. Our carnal eyes are present-moment sighted and God's is all seeing, both the present and the future. He knows you better than you know yourself. For Him to call someone to accomplish a task is never a mistake. He never takes it back. He knows your capabilities, your personality, your flaws, and your shortcomings. He is ready, willing, and able to work with you, correct you, shape your thinking, and mold you into the individual He wants to do the job.

This is not easy. There is a boot-camp time that is spent in what I call the desert. In this place He teaches you the basics of His ways of doing things and how to use the measure of faith you have been dealt. He teaches you to exercise that faith so it will begin to grow. *Without faith it is impossible to please Him* (Hebrews 11:6a). To undertake a calling in God's kingdom requires this faith to be constantly tested and sharpened. This process leaves you as an individual in a position of feeling totally helpless, completely alienated from God and man, presenting itself as a self-destructive mechanism. All the time God is watching your reaction, your faith, and your ability to get along with others during these seemingly crisis times. I always try to remember three promises. One, *I will never leave thee nor forsake thee* (Hebrews 13:5b). Secondly, *I've not seen the righteous forsaken, nor His seed begging for bread* (Psalms 37:25a). Thirdly, *(He) will make a way to escape that you will be able to bear it* (1 Corinthians 10:13b). These scriptures were handy, consoling, and a true lifeline during my five and a half month desert experience.

I heard a man of God say once, "If you don't go through the desert with God as your guide, you have not been called. The ministry you are leading, whether church or para-church, was man called not God called. That calling was either by parents or by you. God has nothing to do with the origination of that ministry. He may bless it if it conforms to the biblical method of living and helping others, but it isn't God called."

After the desert is over, there is a constant training ground on which you will tread. All the lessons are never learned and perfection is never achieved. He has a way about Him that if you stumble and/or fall, He is always, without fail, there to rescue you. The road will be long and difficult. He never promises nor does He provide simplicity. There is always a lesson to be learned, faith to be exercised, or just learning to be dependent on Him and not people.

A great difficulty in leading a God-called ministry, no matter what type, is developing the attitude that God's will is priority number one regardless of people. "People" means everyone from spouse, children, extended family, employees and friends, to those you don't know. Leverages such as money, a powerful leverage, should never be considered in any decision-making regarding the ministry. It is best to listen politely, weigh the facts, test the spirit, and ask God. You will get an answer. Sometimes it is one you like, sometimes it isn't, but you will get an answer. Sometimes the answer is no answer at all. When I get those types of non-answers, I probably should not have asked the question in the first place. Your only option is to simply wait upon the Lord. In His timing you will know your answer.

There will definitely be people, including employees, Board of Directors members, and people in whom you confided and trusted who always know more than you about how the ministry God called you to accomplish should operate. Be very careful where you place your trust. Ask God to reveal to you the individuals to deal with or the circumstances that need to be changed. Ask God to deal with the problem. He will do a much more thorough job than you and will prevent discord and hard feelings. Always remember a ministry called by God cannot have two leaders. A two-headed ministry is not a ministry; it is a monster.

There are those that practically demand you do certain things to suit them. Sometimes threats will even be made. People will compare you to the way others operate and expect you to do the same. There are the ugly phone calls where people blast you, then very impolitely slam the phone in your ear. There are those that will literally curse you for not doing something they selfishly wanted or you may have done something they didn't want you to do. You will come in contact with a number of religious, self-centered, self-righteous individuals that will be nice to your face but cut you to shreds behind your back. All of these types are there. They were there in Jesus' day and our day is no different. How do you deal with this type of action? You don't. You learn to be polite if confronted or overlook the phone call or unsigned letter when received. The scripture plainly states we should pray for those that spitefully use us. Pray for them, their safety, and their attitude. Most of the time these are Christians, but their fruit is tarnished. The fruit has a bruised or rotten spot on the skin. God can deal with, correct, and perfect that fruit. Also remember God says vengeance is His, not ours, although at times you would love to take revenge on the person or persons that wronged you.

You must always remember in any ministry there are business decisions and procedures that should be followed. The decisions and procedures should never interfere with the ministry aspect and definitely not the calling and purpose of the ministry. God knows these rules, and He will not instruct you in a direction that would result in a violation of these rules. More often than not, He will remind you of rules or direct you in such a path that you will discover a violation or potential violation of ministry rules or government regulations. This has happened more than once during the time Immanuel Broadcasting has been on the air, and I have been forever grateful. It saved us a lot of heartache and grief.

There is a price that must be paid to be in the ministry. The enemy is always lurking at the door never to leave you alone. A minister asked me once if I thought the devil was going to sit comfortably under the old oak tree and let Immanuel Broadcasting blast the gospel of Jesus Christ into the very domain he occupies. If I did then I was sadly mistaken. He is going to try and destroy you, the ministry, and everyone involved with it. I may as well prepare myself, put on the armor, and move forward to accomplish that which God has said for me to do, always in the name of Jesus Christ.

Always remember it was God who called you. If you are married, He also called your spouse. You two are a team. Nobody else has a right or a place in the leadership role of that ministry until God says, "WELL DONE MY GOOD AND FAITHFUL SERVANT. ENTER INTO THE JOY OF THE LORD," calling you home for the last calling and the last journey He will ever ask you to go on.

ISBN 155395272-3